GUARDIANS
—OF THE—
UNIVERSE?

GUARDIANS
—OF THE—
UNIVERSE?
RONALD STORY

ST. MARTIN'S PRESS

NEW YORK

Library of Congress Cataloging in Publication Data

Story, Ronald.
    Guardians of the universe?

    Bibliography: p.
    Includes index.
    1.   Civilization, Ancient—Extraterrestrial in-
fluences.   2.   Unidentified flying objects.   3.   Life
on other planets.   4.   Däniken, Erich von, 1935-
I.   Title.
CB156.S75   001.9′4   79-27769
ISBN 0-312-35216-6

To my children:
Brenda and Brian,
with love

CONTENTS

This picture of a God 'out there' coming to earth like some visitor from outer space underlies every popular presentation of the Christian drama of salvation, whether from the pulpit or the presses . . .

. . . there is a ready-made public for whom this whole frame of reference still presents no difficulties . . .

John A. T. Robinson,
Bishop of Woolwich,
Honest to God (*1963*)

PREFACE

Stan Lee, publisher of *Marvel* comics, once said, 'Nowhere else but in comic books can you still recapture the fairy tale fun of finding characters bigger than life, plots wilder than any movie, and good guys battling bad guys with the fate of entire galaxies hanging on the outcome.'* Lee was *almost* right. He overlooked, however, the modern fad of 'adult fantasy' books, as they are sometimes called, that have taken the world by storm.

Leading the hit parade is an ex-hotel manager (and ex-convict) from Switzerland – the irrepressible Erich von Däniken – who has become, over the last ten years, one of the most successful authors of all time. His six books (see Bibliography) have been translated into thirty-five different languages and have sold an astonishing *forty-two million* copies.

His basic 'theory' can be simply put: that superbeings from outer space came to Earth in the distant past, created humans *in their image*, and then founded civilisation on Earth as we know it.

Let me say at the outset that I have no objection to honest speculation. Nor do I find anything impossible about the basic idea that alien beings *could have* visited the Earth in ancient times. But I have found that if you take von Däniken's 'indications' or 'proofs', as he alternately calls them, and subject them to the normal rules of evidence – and generally accepted canons of logic – they fall apart. In other words, from the standpoint of 'proof', or even from the standpoint of a reasoned argument, von Däniken simply does *not* have a case.

Arizona Daily Star, 27 July 1975.

For one thing, the level of technology required for the construction of the various artifacts and monuments in question *never* exceeds the capacities of Earthmen working on their own in the normal context of their own cultures. The archaeological 'wonders' that are alleged to *prove* man's extraterrestrial origins are almost never described correctly and, in the vast majority of cases, what are represented as 'unsolved mysteries of the past' are *not* mysteries at all! It is just that the legitimate facts, which would go contrary to von Däniken's 'theory' if known, are either ignored or suppressed.

Many of the supposed 'proofs' take the form of psychological projective tests (known to psychologists as Rorshach tests) in which the subject (the reader in this case) spontaneously calls out whatever object comes to mind when confronted with an ambiguous shape. But instead of ink blots, von Däniken substitutes ancient art and artifacts. He likes to play the game 'it looks like', as if it were a Rorshach test, but cheats by planting a suggestion in the reader's mind from the very start – suggesting, furthermore, that any alternative interpretation, other than what he has 'suggested', is effectively ruled out.

In my previous book, *The Space-Gods Revealed* (New English Library, 1977), I examined in some detail von Däniken's earlier works, and will be referring the reader to that source, throughout the present book, for a fuller view of those matters that have been previously discussed therein.

In the present book, I will amplify some of those topics not dealt with in sufficient detail previously, and shall attempt to elucidate certain other matters that were not covered at all in *Space-Gods*. Hopefully, I shall also convey the openness which I hold toward the UFO evidence which, in my opinion, is a matter to be taken seriously. Whereas the theories of von Däniken (ie, that alien intervention is needed to explain the evolution of man and human civilisation) rest on either contrived and/or irrational grounds, numerous UFO reports have been verified as real experiences of honest and reliable people. And whereas the solutions to von Däniken's 'mysteries' are actually known to earth scientists, whatever is behind the phenomenon of UFOs is not.

I shall also point out, in Chapter Eleven, what I consider to be possible evidence of ancient UFOs, which seems more plausible to me than the examples which von Däniken has chosen to publish. So that the reader is not confused, my own viewpoint may be summarised as follows: objectivity and open-mindedness should reign supreme, but with a high degree of prudence based on the body of hard-won scientific knowledge that we already possess. Shoddy evidence and apparent deceptions should be weeded out, wherever found, and not confused with reasonable thinking on unorthodox subjects.

Despite what many readers are bound to think, I am not out to 'crucify' von Däniken as a person; but rather, it is the particular brand of irrationality which he represents that I feel is potentially dangerous. He uses *propaganda* (known as the 'informal fallacies' in logic), not reason. Were a much larger segment of humanity to give up its reasoning powers in favour of a blind will-to-believe, we would certainly be in a most vulnerable state. I do not believe in blatant exploitation of human ignornace and gullibility. This is why I want to expose the pseudosciences by bringing to the light of day some of the many little-known facts of science that have for too long been the sole property of scholars and librarians. My books represent an attempt to rescue some of this information from obscurity and place it in the hands of those who care to know.

RONALD D. STORY
March 1979
Tucson, Arizona, USA

ACKNOWLEDGEMENTS

Since the publication of *The Space-Gods Revealed*, three years ago, I have benefited from acquaintances and discussions with many interesting people: interviewers, correspondents, lecture audiences, and two individuals in particular, to whom I owe a special debt: Erich von Däniken himself, without whom, ironically, my own books would not have been possible, and Dr Clifford Wilson (see illus 1), whose pioneering best-seller, *Crash Go the Chariots* (1972), gave me encouragement in my own attempt to set the record straight.

Although Dr Wilson, a Biblical fundamentalist, understandably blasts von Däniken on theological grounds, I felt that the subject of alleged 'Space-Gods' should be exposed, as well, in the light of our abundant scientific knowledge, which has been either distorted or ignored altogether by the current generation of pseudoscience writers.

Among those who helped me to obtain that knowledge are: my Brazilian colleague and correspondent, Fernando G. Sampaio, author of *A Verdade Sobre Os Deuses Astronautas* (*The Truth About the God-Astronauts*, 1973), particularly for material contained in Chapters Five and Ten; Mr J. Bernard Delair, of Contact (UK) International, for material on the late Harold T. Wilkins, which appears in Chapter Two; and various staff members of the University of Arizona as follows: Mr J. Richard Greenwell, research coordinator at the Office of Arid Lands Studies, for reviewing the entire manuscript and for agreeing to provide the article entitled 'Tiptoeing Beyond Darwin' as an

13

Appendix to this book; and, in the Department of Anthropology, Dr Mary Ellen Morbeck, a specialist in human and primate evolution, particularly for suggestions relative to Chapter Four, and Dr William L. Rathje, a Mesoamerican archaeologist, for comments and suggestions relative to Chapter Five.

For translating into English many key pieces of information, available only in foreign languages, I wish to thank my friend Mr Tomás B. Ettrick (for his skilful translations from Spanish and Portuguese), and Mr Richard Achzehner (for his expert translations from French sources).

Small portions of this book have appeared previously as part of an article entitled 'Von Däniken's Golden Gods', in *The Zetetic* (renamed *The Skeptical Inquirer*, the journal of the Committee for the Scientific Investigation of Claims of the Paranormal), in the Fall/Winter 1977 issue.

Every reasonable effort has been made to credit the sources of all illustrations in this book, but, if any credits have been inadvertently omitted, proper corrections and/or additions will be made in future editions.

1 THE VON DÄNIKEN MYSTIQUE

Erich Anton von Däniken (see illus 2) was born on 14 April 1935 in Zofingen, Switzerland. He is not a 'German professor' as was claimed in the television special *In Search of Ancient Astronauts* (first aired in the United States on NBC-TV, 5 January 1973).* Von Däniken is in fact an 'autodidact' (or self-taught man), as his editor Wilhelm Utermann (pen name: Roggersdorf) so kindly put it. More accurately, he is what Americans term a 'high-school dropout', having finished only three years of secondary school at the former Jesuit College of Saint-Michel in Fribourg,

*The exact words were:

> Erich von Däniken, a German professor possessed of the mind of a scientist and the imagination of a romantic, wrote a book called *Chariots of the Gods?* He stated that, sometime in the distant past, man was visited by intelligent beings from outer space. What in olden times might have been heresy is today intriguing speculation. Von Däniken travelled to all corners of the world gathering evidence in support of his theory.

I would also like to point out that the advertisements for the movie, *Chariots of the Gods?*, give no indication that it is intended as fantasy or pure entertainment. The movie poster flatly states that the film is based on 'THE BOOK THAT SHATTERED CONVENTIONAL THEORIES OF HISTORY AND ARCHAEOLOGY!' To say that the book questioned conventional theories might be more accurate – 'shattered' is evidently a piece of publicists' hyperbole which of course went unquestioned by the general public.

Switzerland. He was removed from the school at the age of seventeen by his father and apprenticed to a Swiss hotelier. The young von Däniken did not get on well with his instructors at the school and considered the whole situation at Saint-Michel 'repressive'.

In particular, there were serious disagreements on important religious matters. Von Däniken considered himself an inquiring spirit, whose constant questioning of Catholic doctrine did not sit well with the Church. Erich's father, Otto von Däniken, Sr, was a pious man who became somewhat disappointed with his son, in view of Erich's radical approach to religious matters, and has remained so ever since.

To this day, Erich cites 'religious uncertainty' as a major reason for the success of his books, and 'religious doubts' as his primary motivation for writing them. Fittingly enough, he also claims a vision or ESP experience, allegedly occurring in the Spring of 1954, by which he was impelled to begin a life-long search for traces of the 'gods'. When asked by *Der Spiegel* magazine if ESP were a major source of his knowledge, von Däniken answered: 'A source which led me to the firm belief that the earth had been visited by extra-terrestrial astronauts. I know this. I also know that an event will take place in the near future which will prove I'm right.'[1] Describing his ESP experiences, he said: 'One makes a sort of "journey through time". I step out of time, so I stand outside time and see everything simultaneously – past, present, and future.'[2]

As a young boy (in February 1944), von Däniken had an experience that some psychiatrists feel may have influenced his later thinking. A short distance from his home, an American bomber made an emergency landing. As the young von Däniken looked on, eight men in their flight suits climbed out and walked silently past him, 'like creatures from another world'.[3] Von Däniken himself rejects the notion that this experience had anything to do with his later beliefs. He also rejects, of course, some other opinions levelled at him by psychiatrists: that he is an habitual liar and a criminal psychopath.[4] (I hasten to add that von Däniken told me personally, in February 1976, that the psychiatrist who made the latter judgement 'has been proved wrong in court'. I therefore think it proper to withhold judgement on the matter.)

Readers of *The Space-Gods Revealed* will know that in his missionary zeal to obtain 'first-hand knowledge' for his first book, von Däniken embezzled over 400,000 Swiss francs as a hotelier to finance his 'expeditions' to Egypt, Lebanon, and North and South America.

It seems that he was truly obsessed with the idea that the Earth had been visited by 'gods' from outer space who left traces for us to find. This missionary zeal is perhaps the prime ingredient of von Däniken's later success.

This runaway enthusiasm of the 'god-seeker' (as biographer Peter Krassa calls him) permeates the pages of his books as an unmistakable hallmark of his style. Not only does he write in a simple fashion, which helps readers to understand his ideas, but his enthusiasm is contagious. It is only natural for most people to *want* to believe him. It becomes difficult to imagine just how someone could be so grossly wrong while apparently *so sure* of being right! And that is precisely the impression that von Däniken and his editor Roggersdorf so carefully create. In addition, there is an unfortunate lack of scientific knowledge among the majority of the world's population. It is a sad but true fact that most public education in the sciences is derived more from science *fiction* novels and movies than from textbooks or even popular science books. Scientific documentaries are a rarity on American television although perhaps more common in England. In the movie theatres, true science would probably have the lowest box-office rating imaginable.

It was in March of 1968 when the first edition of *Chariots of the Gods?* (entitled *Erinnerungen an die Zukunft* in the original German, which translates as 'Memories of the Future') rolled off the German press. By December, it was the number-one best-selling book in West Germany and a similar reception was eventually to greet it in most parts of the world. The timing for the book was perfect. Not only did the publicity of von Däniken's trial help sales locally, but events were happening on a global scale to help launch the Swiss iconoclast on his way.

In the United States, plans were being made, and *publicised heavily* (thereby preparing the populations of the world for what was to come), for the first manned lunar voyages, and this was at the precise juncture in history when von Däniken stepped in. When Apollo 8 and its crew of three American astronauts were brought into millions of living rooms all over the world through the miracle of satellite-television, no one could dispute this historic event. Voyagers into space – a modern-day miracle that had formerly been limited to the science-fiction realm – were no longer a dream. The space age had arrived and from that point on, nothing was impossible – or so it seemed. Then, on 20 July 1969, when Neil Armstrong and Edwin Aldrin stepped out of their landing module onto the lunar surface, history was made again. And, as before, on-board television cameras followed the action for viewers back on Earth. This time, an estimated *700 million* TV viewers (an all-time record) watched, stunned and amazed at this technological feat.

The moon landing was indeed 'a giant leap for mankind' in perhaps more ways than most of us realise. At the very least, it gave proof, once and for all, that we really *were* in the space age. And if we can travel to other worlds in our newly devised space vehicles, why couldn't other beings who have been around longer than us have been doing the same thing? In fact, once speculation begins on this topic, it becomes endless. Everything we've ascribed to God, in our religions of the past, we could equally well ascribe to extremely advanced superbeings from 'out there' in the far reaches of space. There is no question but that such Space-Gods could serve perfectly well as *the great common denominator* to replace the traditional deities of all great religions of the world.

In April 1968, a monumental motion picture, *2001: A Space Odyssey*, was previewed. The film's producer (and co-author, with Arthur C. Clarke, of the screenplay), Stanley Kubrick, had this to say in an interview for *Playboy* magazine:

> I will say that the God concept is at the heart of *2001* – but not any traditional, anthropomorphic image of God. I don't believe in any of Earth's monotheistic religions, but I do believe that one can construct an intriguing *scientific* definition of God . . . The important point is that all the standard

attributes assigned to God in our history could equally well be the characteristics of biological entities who, billions of years ago, were at a stage of development similar to man's own and evolved into something as remote from man as man is remote from the primordial ooze from which he first emerged.[5]

Von Däniken's first book not only expressed a similar theme to the film *2001*, but, in addition, was made credible by the actual achievements of the real astronauts. The world was ready and waiting and the public got just what it was primed for.

There are, of course, other reasons for the blind popularity of the Space-God theory. After all, it is basically a *fun* thing to believe. Marvellous beings from another planet with super-human powers, swooping down out of the sky to create human beings and civilisation as we know it. Archaeologists cannot hold a candle to the kind of entertainment value offered by books and movies exploiting this theme. And the added possibility that the Space-Gods might return one day offers *hope* for the future – a psychological necessity during these critical times.

Just ask yourself: how popular would Jesus Christ be in the Christian religion without the belief in his eventual *return* to this Earth? If he were just an ancient teacher of wisdom, like Socrates or Plato for instance, buried in a grave and gone for ever, would he hold the same level of interest? Obviously not – and that is the crucial point. There is no apparent salvation in past genera-tions of stone-carvers or clever city-builders who are dead and gone. But if ancient 'astronauts' were involved, perhaps, many of us reason (either consciously or unconsciously), they may come back some day to help us once again. The essential idea is conveyed by the catch phrase used in ads for the movie *Close Encounters of the Third Kind* – 'We Are Not Alone'.

The very concept of God that most of us have been taught consists of this familiar mental image: God is a superbeing from a super-world from somewhere 'out there' (ie among the stars). This whole frame of reference fits perfectly the theme that God is an astronaut.

Another feat accomplished by von Däniken was *seemingly* to reconcile modern science with a literal interpretation of the Bible.

19

Speculations are generally more popular anyway, if they are overly simple. Abstruse theology is just as forbidding to many people as is academic science. The real answer to a difficult problem oftentimes requires more mental effort than many are willing or able to muster.

But I think the real 'icing on the cake' for von Däniken, that placed him above the feeble efforts of his many predecessors, was his claim of *proof* – which, incidentally, is the intended theme of his latest work, entitled *According to the Evidence: My Proof of Man's Extraterrestrial Origins* (1978).

In the present book, as in *The Space-Gods Revealed*, we shall examine carefully the most famous examples of alleged 'evidence' and 'proof' that von Däniken offers in support of 'his theory'; but, as was not done previously, we shall take more of an in-depth look at some of his important predecessors, without whom the best-selling author would not have known the many 'mysteries' he writes about.

SOURCE NOTES

1 Reprinted in the British periodical, *Encounter*, August 1973, p11.
2 Ibid., p11.
3 Ibid., p14.
4 *Playboy*, August 1974, p51.
5 *Playboy*, September 1968, pp94 and 96.

2 OTHER GOD-SEEKERS

It is said that Madame Helena Petrovna Blavatsky (1831–91), founder of the spiritualist cult called 'Theosophy', taught that man is not a genuine native of this Earth. In *The Secret Doctrine*, published in 1888, she promoted such themes as Atlantis, Lemuria, and multiple planes of existence. Although it is not clear just how many ideas von Däniken borrowed from her, she is cited by him as a source. Her successor, Annie Besant, is credited with the theory that civilisations on Earth developed with the aid of teachers from Venus.

Another famous pioneer of the alien-visitation theory to account for UFOs and other bizarre mysteries (both real and manufactured) was Charles Hoy Fort (1974–1932). Fort was a former newspaper reporter and amateur naturalist who, for over two decades, collected stories of strange, unexplained events ignored by science, for which he would propose various exotic solutions, some tongue-in-cheek, some seriously. One of his favourite such hypotheses was that the Earth might be 'owned' by superior beings from another planet, who check up on us from time to time. 'We are property,' he would say, just like a farmer owns his pigs, cattle, and sheep. And, similarly, we don't realise it. Fort also seemed to hold the same contempt for astronomers that von Däniken has displayed for archaeologists. Both authors depict scientists in general as stumblebums who can't see the obviously correct solutions to some of the greatest mysteries on our planet. Although von Däniken may not have copied Fort in any direct way, Fort must be included, nevertheless, in any attempt to trace the historical origins of the ancient astronaut theory. Von Däniken fits squarely in Fortean tradition (perhaps to the dismay of many contemporary Forteans).

Much has appeared in the media concerning alleged plagiarism by von Däniken of other writers who had advanced similar ideas years before him. (I have prepared a chronological list of the most notable of them, which starts on this page.) It is with good reason that plagiarism was suspected. First is the fact that von Däniken avoided naming his sources (corrections were later made in reprinted editions of his first book), so it is natural to wonder why?

Famous among these forerunners are the French authors Louis Pauwels, Jacques Bergier, and the late Robert Charroux (pen name of Robert Grugeau, 1909–78). Published in 1960, *The Morning of the Magicians*, by Pauwels and Bergier, was a 'classic' in this field, which contained numerous examples of parallel 'evidence', which found their way into von Däniken's books. One of Charroux's books, called *One Hundred Thousand Years of Man's Unknown History* (first published in 1963), was almost a 'blueprint' for *Chariots of the Gods?* (See *The Space-Gods Revealed*, p5, for a partial list of the specific parallels.)

EARLY PROPONENTS OF THE SPACE-GOD THEORY:

Helena Petrovna Blavatsky	late 1800s
Annie Besant	early 1900s
Charles Fort	,, ,,
Richard S. Shaver	early 1940s
Desmond Leslie	early 1950s
George Adamski	,, ,,
Harold T. Wilkins	,, ,,
Morris K. Jessup	,, ,,
George Hunt Williamson (pen name for Michel d'Obrenovic)	late 1950s
M. M. Agrest	,, ,,
Jacques Bergier	early 1960s
Louis Pauwels	,, ,,
Robert Charroux (pen name for Robert Grugneau)	,, ,,
Brinsley Le Poer Trench	,, ,,
Aleksandr Kazântsev	,, .,,

W. Raymod Drake	early 1960s
Paul Thomas (pen name for Paul Misraki)	,, ,,
John Michell	mid 1960s
Otto Binder	,, ,,
Max Flindt	,, ,,
Jean Sendy	,, ,,

There were earlier books also and scattered magazine articles which contained most of von Däniken's other 'evidence', which will be mentioned in turn as each specific example of alleged 'proof' is considered later in this book.

The British author Harold T. Wilkins (c 1883–1960) certainly deserves a mention as one of the early pioneers of the ancient astronaut theory. Educated at Cambridge, where Wilkins excelled at languages, little is known of his early career. After the First World War, however, he entered journalism and, among other things, developed a keen interest in archaeology. In due course, he produced books on 'lost cities' and other 'mysteries' of South America, before the coming of the 'flying saucer' age. From 1947 onwards, Wilkins quickly developed a deep interest in this subject and, with considerable assistance from his earlier journalist contacts, built up a remarkable record of early UFO activity. His files and collection of UFO-related newspaper cuttings (in many languages) constituted the first great collection of its kind in Britain. (The greater part of this collection is now in the archives of a UFO organisation called Contact International, based in Richmond, Surrey, England.) Much of this material formed the basis of his two published books about UFOs: *Flying Saucers From the Moon* (published in the United States as *Flying Saucers on the Attack*, 1954) and *Flying Saucers Uncensored* (1955).

In *Flying Saucers on the Attack*, Wilkins wrote that '*our earth may have been under observation by extra-terrestrial visitants for some 1250 years past*' (italics in the original),[1] and that the mysterious lines on the desert at Nazca might have been '*indications to an interplanetary space ship* [of] *where to land*' (italics in the original).[2] Probably *the* most important pioneer in this field (the pseudoscience of ancient astronauts), from the standpoints of impact and relevance, is the late astronomer-explorer, Morris K. Jessup (1900–59). Jessup (see illus 3) was the *first* writer with legitimate academic credentials (he received his Master of Science degree from the University of Michigan, in 1926, and was an instructor in astronomy there), to take the Space-God theory seriously, which he offered as a working hypothesis in his first book, *The Case for the UFO* (1955).

In addition to his research in astronomy, Jessup was engaged in archaeological studies of the Maya in the jungles of Central America (for the Carnegie Institute of Washington, DC) and carried out independent investigations of the Inca ruins of Peru – contending that the stonework he found there had been erected by the levitating power of spaceships in antediluvian times. In his Preface to *The Case for the UFO*, Jessup wrote: 'There is one sphere of indirect evidence in the form of events of mysterious nature which have never been explained. These things would be easy to explain were we to admit the limitations of our own knowledge, and the possibility of "intelligence" elsewhere in the universe operating space ships . . .' Does this approach sound familiar?

In the same book, Jessup speaks of 'erratics of archaeology' and 'remnants of cultures of almost unspeakable age'. And although he invokes the aid of Space-Gods to explain such mysteries in his book, one is surprised to find in some of his earlier writings more conventional explanations for some of the same 'wonders'. Due to this sharp contrast in point of view – between the early Jessup and the late Jessup – I cannot resist reprinting, in full, a short article of his that appeared in the May 1949 issue of *Fate* magazine:

THE INCA'S SECRET SOLVED

For years the Inca's skill in constructing stone walls without mortar, so perfectly a knife blade could not be inserted in the cracks, has baffled us. Here is the answer.

Away back in the dim days, not only beyond the recall of civilisations now existing, but ancient even before the first white man set foot on the Americas, a powerful race of men lived in the lofty vastness of the high Andes. Everyone knows about the Incas of Peru and the fabulous wealth which was taken from them through torture by the Spaniards. Few, however, know that much of their famous stone work was built on foundations laid by a race, mythical in its antiquity, of which so little is known that practically the only description which can be given them is implied in the one phrase: 'pre-Inca'.

Most of us have read or heard that the Incas were a race of stonecutters whose skill was much greater than that of present-day craftsmen. So great was their skill, so we are told, that they were able to quarry stones and cut them to such a fine precision that they not only fitted perfectly but needed no cement to hold them together. It is also told, and accurately, that much of the Inca masonry is so close fitting that even a thin knife blade cannot be thrust into the joints.

Less familiar, however, is the fact that there are single stones in some of the walls weighing fifty tons or more. Or that there are still larger masses of stone weighing perhaps one or two hundred tons, which show every sign of having been torn from the mountainsides by geologic forces *after* they had had stairways, rooms, and passages cut in them by human hands.

There is an observatory to which scientists have attributed an age of at least thirteen thousand years, based on astronomical evidence. There is evidence that the Incas quarried stone from the shattered remains of masonry work which must have been made by people who had flourished thousands of years before them.

In attributing such phenomenal skill to the Inca stonecutters, we are but falling into an error common to our ways of thinking. Because we quarry our stone and cut it to shape before making our walls, we assume that the Inca did the same thing. However, the stonecutting of the Incas needed no complex or mystical tools of hard metal, formed by a lost art, as many explorers have claimed. We have attributed to the Inca an intelligence inferior to our own and a skill much greater than that of our modern masons. Actually the Inca, lacking our tools and likewise our skill, produced a miracle of wall-building through the sheer brain power to take a short cut.

The Inca stones were not pre-cut to specified sizes and dimensions. Instead they were rough-quarried, when quarried at all, and then ground to a perfect fit, *in situ*. The Inca potentate building a new palace or store house was thus able to make use of unskilled labour throughout, and without the aid of an engineering staff or complex blueprints, so necessary to present-day structural projects. In fact, so simple was the process that the emperor could possibly have found time to oversee the work himself.

How do we know this? Easy. The stones in the Inca walls are cut to very irregular shapes, few are rectangular, many have concavities and 'inside corners'. One stone actually has twelve corners, or angles, counting inside and outside ones. But – and here is the little thing that gives away the secret – there are no corners concave *downward*. In every case of a concave, or inside, corner there is perfect evidence that the stone above was worked into place by grinding under its own weight. So simple!

In the earliest walls very irregular stones were used. Probably they were loose boulders or, if quarried, were hacked out crudely. Later walls show remarkable development in skill, however. The latest walls were made of a red stone cut to approximate shape in large slabs nearly a foot thick and four feet long. Each shows perfect fitting at the joints, and at each joint there is a tiny protruberance from the upper stone into the minute space between the two lower stones – the never-failing telltale showing that even these were worked into their final perfect fit by grinding, aided by the force of gravity.

Now, instead of imagining an army of skilled stonecutters, each spending years working at a few stones of predetermined shape, it is easy to picture a horde of unskilled labourers lined up along a wall. The bottom tier of rocks has been set into the ground and another tier of rough or semi-finished stones laid on top. The entire group of workers, perhaps hundreds in number, are slowly pushing stones back and forth, perhaps pouring on a little water and sand now and then. And, who knows, maybe whole buildings went up to the rhythm of mountain music not far removed from the style of modern hillbilly!

26

For such a construction there is no need to envision hopeless slaves driven by cruel and heartless masters under a torrid tropical sun, as we have imagined heretofore in the case not only of the Incas, but of the Egyptians and other races whose stone structures have been marvels in magnitude and magnificence. Instead, the buildings of the Incas could be the outcome of civic pride under the direction of a benign monarch, and the work done by a socialised community in the seasons between crops. The magnitude of the Inca stone work is not appalling when considered in this light.

There are those who have tried to connect the mystical images of Easter Island and the stone platforms on which they rest with the masons of early Peru. Certain resemblances in the walls have been noted in a vague way. Perhaps a more detailed inspection would tell whether the joints at Easter Island were made by grinding, *in situ*, with the aid of gravity. If so, would not this unique method identify the makers with the masons of the Incas?

Some time between 1949 and 1955, Jessup apparently changed his mind. No longer would such a prosaic explanation be satisfactory to explain such mysteries. In *The Case for the UFO* he suggests something far more exciting:

I have used the word 'levitation' as a substitute for power or force. I have suggested that *flying saucers* used some means of reacting with the gravitational field. In this way they could apply accelerations or lifting forces to all particles of a body, inside and outside, simultaneously, and not through external force applied by pressure, or harness, to the surface only. I believe that this same, or a similar force was used to move stones in very ancient times. I believe the source of this lifting or levitating power was lost suddenly.

We believe, in short, that this lifting engine was a space ship, probably of vast proportions; that it brought colonists to various parts of the earth, probably from other terrestrial areas; and that it supplied the heavy-lift power for erecting great stone works; and that it was suddenly destroyed, or taken

27

away. Such a hypothesis would underwrite all of the movements of stone over which archaeologists and engineers have puzzled.[3]

Jessup was also one of the first to publish speculations on UFOs in the Bible, the specifics of which will be presented later on, as our story unfolds. As can be seen already, Jessup used a similar form of reasoning and the same general categories of evidence as von Däniken after him.

Another noteworthy pioneer of the Space-God theory is the British author W[alter] Raymond Drake. Drake's *Gods and Spacemen* series of books (see Bibliography) represents the most thorough treatment of the subject by any author, representing the 'pro' side of the ancient-astronaut controversy prior to von Däniken. Drake's articles were first published, in 1957, in Ray Palmer's magazine *Flying Saucers*, and the book *Gods or Spacemen?* (Amherst Press) was likewise published by Palmer in 1964. (It is probably no accident that the late Ray Palmer was best known as a writer, editor, and publisher of *science fiction*.)

Another Englishman whose articles appeared in Palmer's magazine is Brinsley Le Poer Trench, now the eighth Earl of Clancarty. Trench served as editor of the British *Flying Saucer Review* from 1956 to 1959 and wrote seven books (see Bibliography) on UFOs and ancient astronauts, the earliest of which was: *The Sky People*, published in 1960. More will be said about Trench in the next chapter.

There have been others, as well, who have written and published prior to von Däniken along similar lines; most of whom will be credited throughout this book as we consider the fantastic claims of 'evidence' and even alleged 'proof' of 'gods from outer space'.

Source Notes

1 Harold T. Walkins, *Flying Saucers on the Attack* (New York: Citadel Press, 1954), p157.
2 Ibid., p160.
3 M. K. Jessup, *The Case for the UFO* (New York: Citadel Press, 1955), p152.

3 GOD AS ASTRONAUT*

According to Raymond Drake, writing in *Gods or Spacemen?* (1964),

> The strongest evidence of all proving the existence of the Space Beings and their war with earthly Giants [a scenario adopted by von Däniken] is surely to be found in our Bible in the Book of Genesis . . . If Genesis means what it so plainly says, the Lord was no intangible spirit or the voice of conscience but a powerful Being, a Spaceman, with squadrons of winged globes or fiery wheels.[1]

Much of von Däniken's broad appeal derives, I think, from his use of the Bible as an authority symbol while at the same time reinterpreting the scriptures to suit his own needs. Amazingly, he seems to reconcile modern science with a literal interpretation of the Bible. He creates the illusion that the Bible is really just a straightforward account of spaceships landing and spacemen trotting all over the place, to give his audience everything it wants – Biblical truth combined with exciting adventures akin to Buck Rogers or Flash Gordon, presented as historical fact – without the requirement that anyone need do a great deal of thinking. As mentioned earlier, von Däniken's speculations are fun, which adds to his appeal.

So, what do we find when we look at the Bible anew with our

*In his fifth book, *Miracles of the Gods*, von Däniken writes: 'It is staggering that the fairy tale of the Bible as "God's word" has endured so long . . .' (London: Corgi Books, 1977, p54).

'space eyes', which we have acquired from Jessup, Trench, Drake and von Däniken? In his book *UFO and the Bible*, Jessup sees it this way: 'If we can manage to shake off the creeping paralysis called sophistication,' he says, 'and make a reinterpretation of the straightforward statements in the Bible, based on *reasonable postulates of space-life and space-intelligence, we shall have gone very far toward a reconciliation of science and religion.*'[2] According to Jessup, 'The existence of space-intelligence, relatively near the earth, but yet away from it and in open space, and the probability of a super-race using navigable contrivances, fits all conditions which we have been able to attribute to UFOs, and thus rationalises scriptural events.'[3] As specific examples, Jessup cites the teleportation of Elijah in a 'fiery chariot', 'angels', who appeared in flames and in clouds, the ascension of Jesus into the clouds, the wheel of Ezekiel, the pillar of cloud (and pillar of fire) followed by Moses, and others. (Specific passages will be given from the Bible as each example is considered later, in detail.)

Brinsley Le Poer Trench expanded upon Jessup's notions in his book *The Sky People*, published a few years later (in 1960). Trench went a little further in his analysis of specifics, as the following summary of his views suggests:

(1) The gods and goddesses of Greek, Roman, and Hebrew mythology, who allegedly had contact with mortal human beings, were really extraterrestrials (or the Sky People).

(2) The Hebrew version of the Old Testament refers to the Sky People when it uses the plural term *Elohim*, which translates as *gods*. Therefore, there must have been more than one God who created the Heaven and the Earth (Genesis 1:1).

(3) Chemical Earth-animal man or Adam-II humanity (Trench's terminology) was created by Jehovah, who was one of the Elohim.

(4) This event occurred on the planet Mars, the real location of the Garden of Eden.

(5) Jehovah, who was originally a Lord of Mars, was 'cast out of Heaven' and brought some of Adam-II humanity to Earth. This event is referred to in the Old Testament as the story of

Noah and the Ark. Noah was actually Jehovah, and his ark was a spaceship.

(6) The flood in the story of Noah was probably due to the sudden melting of the northern Martian polar cap.

(7) The destruction of Sodom and Gomorrah, in which fire and brimstone rained out of Heaven, was probably a nuclear explosion set off by the Sky People.

(8) The Ten Commandments given to Moses were a gift from Jehovah who landed on Mount Sinai in a 'flying saucer'.

(9) Jesus was fathered by Gabriel (a Galactic man of the Adam-I line) and not through sexual intercourse, but through a process of using his voice and mind.

(10) The Star of Bethlehem was, what else but, a spaceship.

Although differing in certain matters of detail, von Däniken's Biblical exegesis follows the *general* trend of these writers, such as Jessup, Trench, and Drake, before him. Let us now examine, in some detail, the case of the 'Biblical astronauts' as argued by von Däniken himself.

ELOHIM

In *Chariots of the Gods?* von Däniken quotes the Book of Genesis wherein it says: 'And God said, let us make man in our image, after our likeness' (1:26). And he asks, 'Why does God speak in the plural?' Surely, he reasons, this could only mean that a group of gods (=spacemen) were.involved, suggesting intervention by extraterrestrials.

Actually, the Hebrew version of the Old Testament uses the word *Elohim*, which is gramatically a plural form, translated as God in the English Bible. However, certain passages of the English version retain the plural form, such as the passage (1:26) quoted above, and the phrase 'Behold the man is become as one of us' (Genesis 3:22).

It is well known among Bible scholars that Elohim represents the 'royal we' or plural of majesty, although polytheism cannot be entirely ruled out. It must also be realised that it was customary, at the time the scriptures were written, to view the supreme Deity as a Lord in the company of his subordinate angels. This 'heavenly court' might well be the intention of the reference in the plural, but even so, need not refer to a landing party of spacemen. In short, the literalist interpretation of von Däniken and like-minded writers is patently naïve and ignores true Biblical scholarship in favour of preconceived ideas.

GIANTS

References to the 'sons of God' and 'giants' provide another example of von Däniken's lack of sophistication in understanding the Bible. The passage he quotes is the following:

'There were giants in the earth in those days; and also after that, when the sons of God came in unto the daughters of men, and they bore children to them, the same became mighty men which were of old, men of renown' (Genesis 6:4).[4] For von Däniken this passage represents a clear case of bestiality, between a race of physical giants (=spacemen) and prehistoric ape-women, who were found on Earth at the time. The result was the first race of *Homo sapiens* – our ancestors – who went on to spread humanity throughout the world. 'Who can tell us what sons of God took the daughters of men to wife?' von Däniken asks. 'Where do the "sons of God" come from?'[5]

According to *The Interpreter's Dictionary of the Bible*, the 'sons of God' were indeed 'heavenly beings' but '. . . simply a mythological relic, like Cupid or the Muses in English poetry'.[6] Von Däniken often denies that much of the Bible was meant to be read symbolically – or at least allegorically. *The Oxford Annotated Bible* has it that 'The birth of the Nephilim [giants] is related to demonstrate the increase of wickedness on the earth.'[7] Von Däniken states confidently: 'Giants haunt the pages of almost all ancient books. So they must have existed.'[8] Nothing could better illustrate his faulty method of reasoning, wherein he commits the fallacy in logic called the *non sequitur*. Because giants are mentioned in ancient books it *does not* necessarily mean that 'they must have existed'. The authors of *The Inter-*

preter's Bible consider the 'giants' in the Bible, as in some other ancient books, 'an ancient fantasy that is inconsistent with the higher faith of Genesis'. They say: 'Apparently the compilers included this fragment of an ancient myth because it was too familiar to be ignored.'[9] Certainly, if we were to consider every item of ancient mythology to be literal truth – as von Däniken apparently recommends – we would encounter many outright contradictions and outlandish fantasies that even von Däniken would think absurd. As von Däniken once told me, he has his 'own logic'; with this I certainly agree.

SODOM AND GOMORRAH

In the 22 February 1960 issue of *Time* magazine there appeared an article, entitled 'Enoch & Other Cosmonauts', in which two Russian writers were mentioned in connection with their 'daring new theories', just published in the *Literary Gazette*, the journal of the Soviet Writers Union. The two writers, Valentin Rich and Mikhail Chernenkov, had suggested, for one thing, that the Biblical account of Sodom and Gomorrah might be a literal description of a nuclear explosion set off by alien cosmonauts who wanted to blow up dumps of extra nuclear fuel, of the type used for their spaceship. *Time* called the speculation 'saucer-eyed silliness', eighteen years ago, having no idea how many millions of people in the world of the 1970s would become disciples of Erich von Däniken; an author whose time had not yet come. Yes, the same speculation appears today under von Däniken's byline, just as we might expect.

Again, quoting from *Chariots*:

Let us imagine for a moment that Sodom and Gomorrah were destroyed according to plan, ie deliberately, by a nuclear explosion. Perhaps – let us speculate a little further – the 'angels' simply wanted to destroy some dangerous fissionable material and at the same time to make sure of wiping out a human brood they found unpleasant.[10]

*

33

First of all, let us consult the Bible for the relevant passages that describe the destruction of the two cities:

> And it came to pass, when they had brought them forth abroad, that He [God] said, Escape for thy life; look not behind thee, neither stay thou in all the plain; escape to the mountain, lest thou be consumed (Genesis 19:17).

> Then the Lord rained upon Sodom and Gomorrah brimstone and fire from the Lord out of heaven;
> And he overthrew those cities, and all the plain, and all the inhabitants of the cities, and that which grew upon the ground.
> But his [Lot's] wife looked back from behind him, and she became a pillar of salt (Genesis 19:24, 25, 26).

> And he [Abraham] looked towards Sodom and Gomorrah, and toward all the land of the plain, and beheld, and, lo, the smoke of the country went up as the smoke of a furnace (Genesis 19:28).

Von Däniken says: 'Those who were to escape it such as the Lot family had to stay a few miles from the centre of the explosion in the mountains, for the rock faces would naturally absorb the powerful dangerous rays. And – we all know the story – Lot's wife turned around and looked straight at the atomic sun.'[11]

It so happens that the Biblical passages quoted above do *not* describe what happens in an atomic explosion. There is a first blinding flash of light, followed by a mushroom-shaped cloud, and a shock-wave that would probably not have left the Lot family standing.*

What then could have happened, if we are to believe the Biblical story? Isaac Asimov, in *Asimov's Guide to the Bible* (Vol I), suggests three possibilities: '. . . a volcanic eruption, combined with an earthquake; or, conceivably, a large meteorite

*The interested reader may wish to consult William Laurence's excellent book *Men and Atoms*, Simon and Schuster, New York, 1959, for an eyewitness account of the first nuclear test explosion at Trinity Site, New Mexico, on the morning of 16 July 1945.

strike'.[12] Geophysicists have ruled out volcanic activity, as there is no evidence for such eruptions in the area within the last 4,000 years. As for the meteorite strike, luckily, we do not have to grope that far. Asimov touched on the solution when he mentioned the possibility of an earthquake. In fact, there is strong evidence, indeed, that the Twin Sin Cities felt the wrath of an earthquake, setting off subterranean explosions of natural gas.

The strangeness of the Dead Sea (which is not a sea, but, actually, a great salt lake) has been noted by some of the earliest historians of recorded history (see illus 4). In particular, they mentioned 'slime pits', or natural deposits of oil and asphalt. The Greek geographer Strabo (c 100 BC) wrote that:

[The asphalt] is blown to the surface at irregular intervals from the midst of the deep, and with it rise bubbles, as though the water were boiling . . . With the asphalt there arises also much soot, which, though smoky, is imperceptible to the eye . . . The asphalt is a clod of earth, which at first is liquefied by heat and is blown up to the surface . . . the source of the fire and also the greater part of the asphalt is at the middle of it (Dead Sea); but the bubbling up is irregular, because the movement of the fire, like that of many other subterranean blasts, follows no order known to us.

Many evidences are produced to show that the country is fiery; for near Moasada are to be seen rugged rocks that have been scorched, as also, in many places, fissures and ashy soil, and drops of pitch dripping from smooth cliffs, and boiling rivers that emit foul odours to a great distance, and ruined settlements here and there; and therefore people believe the oft-repeated assertions of the local inhabitants, that there were once thirteen inhabited cities in that region of which Sodom was the metropolis, but that a circuit of about sixty stadia of that city escaped unharmed; and that by reason of earthquakes and of eruptions of fire and hot waters containing asphalt and sulphur, the lake burst its bounds, and rocks were enveloped with fire, and, as for the cities, some were swallowed up and others were abandoned by such as were able to escape.[13]

*

35

It happened that the wicked cities of Sodom and Gomorrah stood over the world's largest earthquake-causing fault, known as the East African Rift or Great Rift Valley System. Spanning a fifth of the Earth's circumference, the vast fault line (which is at some parts fifty miles wide) extends from Bible Lands in the Near East (north) deep into East Africa (at the southern extremity). Earthquakes have been frequent along the Great Rift, and geophysicists have determined that the one that induced the catastrophe at the southern end of the Dead Sea probably occurred around 1900 BC.

EZEKIEL'S WHEELS

Perhaps the favourite item in the Bible of those predisposed towards belief in ancient astronauts is the famous 'wheels' of Ezekiel and attendant 'living creatures' that he allegedly saw. The pertinent Bible verses are as follows:

Now it came to pass in the thirtieth year, in the fourth *month*, in the fifth *day* of the month, as I *was* among the captives by the river of Chebar, *that* the heavens were opened, and I saw visions of God.

In the fifth *day* of the month, which *was* the fifth year of king Jehoiachin's captivity,

The word of the LORD came expressly unto Ezekiel the priest, the son of Buzi, in the land of the Chaldeans by the river Chebar; and the hand of the LORD was there upon him.

And I looked, and, behold, a whirlwind came out of the north, a great cloud, and a fire infolding itself, and a brightness *was* about it, and out of the midst thereof as the colour of amber, out of the midst of the fire.

Also out of the midst thereof *came* the likeness of four living creatures. And this *was* their appearance; they had the likeness of a man.

And every one had four faces, and every one had four wings.

And their feet *were* straight feet; and the sole of their feet *was* like the sole of a calf's foot: and they sparkled like the colour of burnished brass.

And *they had* the hands of a man under their wings on their four sides; and they four had their faces and their wings.

Their wings *were* joined one to another; they turned not when they went; they went every one straight forward.

As for the likeness of their faces, they four had the face of a man, and the face of a lion, on the right side: and they four had the face of an ox on the left side; they four also had the face of an eagle.

Thus *were* their faces: and their wings *were* stretched upward; two *wings* of every one *were* joined one to another, and two covered their bodies.

And they went every one straight forward: whither the spirit was to go, they went; *and* they turned not when they went.

As for the likeness of the living creatures, their appearance *was* like burning coals of fire, *and* like the appearance of lamps: it went up and down among the living creatures; and the fire was bright, and out of the fire went forth lightning.

And the living creatures ran and returned as the appearance of a flash of lightning.

Now as I beheld the living creatures, behold one wheel upon the earth by the living creatures, with his four faces.

The appearance of the wheels and their work *was* like unto the colour of a beryl: and they four had one likeness: and their appearance and their work *was* as it were a wheel in the middle of a wheel.

When they went, they went upon their four sides: *and* they turned not when they went.

As for their wings, they were so high that they were dreadful; and their wings *were* full of eyes round about them four.

And when the living creatures went, the wheels went by them: and when the living creatures were lifted up from the earth, the wheels were lifted up.

Whithersoever the spirit was to go, they went, thither *was their* spirit to go; and the wheels were lifted up over against them: for the spirit of the living creatures *was* in the wheels.

37

When those went, *these* went; and when those stood, *these* stood; and when those were lifted up from the earth, the wheels were lifted up over against them: for the spirit of the living creature *was* in the wheels.

And the likeness of the firmament upon the heads of the living creature *was* as the colour of the terrible crystal, stretched forth over their heads above.

And under the firmament *were* their wings straight, the one towards the other: every one had two, which covered on this side, and every one had two, which covered on that side, their bodies.

And when they went, I heard the noise of their wings, like the noise of great waters, as the voice of the Almighty, the voice of speech, as the noise of an host; when they stood, they let down their wings.

And there was a voice from the firmament that *was* over their heads, when they stood, *and* had let down their wings.

And above the firmament that *was* over their heads *was* the likeness of a throne, as the appearance of a sapphire stone: and upon the likeness of the throne *was* the likeness as the appearance of a man above upon it.

And I saw as the colour of amber, as the appearance of fire round about within it, from the appearance of this loins even upward, and from the appearance of his loins ever downward, I saw as it were the appearance of fire, and it had brightness round about.

As the appearance of the bow that is in the cloud in the day of rain, so *was* the appearance of the brightness round about. This was the appearance of the likeness of the glory of the LORD. And when I saw *it*, I fell upon my face, and I heard a voice of one that spake.

Von Däniken quotes selectively, of course, from the foregoing passages, and it is easy to see how some could rationalise a space vehicle from these words. What is needed, in order to appreciate fully the symbolic significance of Ezekiel's vision, is to view it against a background of the religious ideas of the times.

Ezekiel was a Hebrew priest (and prophet) who received his calling in 593 BC in the experience just related. It is significant that his vision came *from the north*, since in Canaanite mythology, the gods did live in the north. We find in *The Oxford Annotated Bible* that the *living creatures* were cherubim, composite creature-forms derived from Babylonian custom (having come originally from early animal-worship), symbolising mobility, intelligence and strength (see illus 5–10). '*The four wheels* . . . symbolise omni-directional mobility.'[14] Thus, the throne-chariot was intended to symbolise God.

Josef Blumrich, a former engineer at the National Aeronautics and Space Administration (NASA), has written a book entitled *The Spaceships of Ezekiel*, which goes further than von Däniken in more ways than one. The ex-NASA engineer believes, like von Däniken, that Ezekiel's visions were not of God, but of a space-craft piloted by a spaceman whom Ezekiel had confused with God. However, Blumrich doctors up his Biblical quotes just a smidgen to make them conform a little better to his spaceship interpreta-tion. For instance, he gives Ezekiel 1:7 as: 'Their legs were straight, and the soles of their feet were *round*' (emphasis added).[15] Not as von Däniken quoted (and as my own copy of the Bible says): '. . . the sole of their feet was like the sole of a calf's foot . . .' The *round* foot, of course, sounds more like the foot pad of landing gear than a 'calf's foot'.[16] A calf's hoof or the hoof of a horse is round and could certainly have provided Ezekiel with the idea. Another instance of Blumrich's own original translation, as well as interpretation, of Biblical scripture is his quote of Ezekiel 3:12: 'Then the spirit lifted me up, and as the glory of the Lord arose from its place, I heard behind me the sound of a great *earthquake*' (emphasis added).[17] Again, both von Däniken's quote and my Bible disagree. Where Blumrich uses the word 'earthquake', presumably to sound more like a blast-off, even von Däniken quotes the passage as a great 'rushing'.[18]

The Spaceships of Ezekiel, in all honesty, can only be described as an extreme form of rationalisation, with a good supply of technical jargon, charts, and diagrams, carefully designed to impress the general reader. The book does contain a good collection of impressive drawings which prove nothing more than that whoever prepared them is a good draughtsman.

ARK OF THE COVENANT

Perhaps von Däniken's most careless interpretation of all, concerning the Bible, is his claim that the Ark of the Covenant (built by Moses according to exact instructions from God) was an electric condenser. In *Chariots of the Gods?* we are reminded of God's instructions to Moses that:

> No one . . . should come close to the Ark of the Covenant . . . [but] In spite of all this care there was a slip up . . . David had the Ark . . . moved and Uzzah helped to drive the cart it was in. When passing cattle shook and threatened to overturn the Ark, Uzzah grabbed hold of it. He fell dead on the spot, as if struck by lightning.
>
> Undoubtedly the Ark was electrically charged! If we reconstruct it today according to the instructions handed down by Moses, a voltage of several hundred volts is produced. The condenser is formed by the gold plates, one of which is positively, the other negatively, charged.
>
> The details of the construction of the Ark of the Covenant can be read in the Bible in their entirety. Without actually consulting Exodus, I seem to remember that the Ark was often surrounded by flashing sparks . . .[19]

Indeed, one can find the complete list of instructions in the Bible, and nowhere does it describe anything that would produce electricity.* Von Däniken has concocted all of this out of thin air! The Ark was in fact a piece of the tabernacle's furniture, made to

*Clifford Wilson devotes a full chapter to this subject in his book *Crash Go The Chariots*, which includes a 7-page interview (pp43–9) with an electrical expert who explains just exactly why the Ark's specifications do *not* comprise an electrical device.

contain two divine tablets and other holy objects. In other words, a box or oblong chest of shittim (acacia) wood, 2½ cubits long by 1½ cubits broad and deep. It was overlayed with gold, had gold rings in the corners and a mercy seat on top. These and other precise details of its construction are given in Exodus 25:10–28. Hopefully, before believing von Däniken, the wise reader will, in the future, check for himself.

'Without actually consulting Exodus, I seem to remember that the Ark was often surrounded by flashing sparks,' says von Däniken and this statement is shocking in more ways than one. If he *had* consulted Exodus he would have found no such reference. *The Bible does not say the Ark was surrounded by flashing sparks at all!*

Concerning the supposed electrocution of Uzzah, let us examine the pertinent passages in the Bible which von Däniken does not quote:

And when they came to Nachon's threshing floor, Uzzah put forth *his hand* to the ark of God, and took hold of it; for the oxen shook *it*.

And the anger of the LORD was kindled against Uzzah; and God smote him there for *his* error; and there he died by the ark of God (II Samuel 6:6–7).

In his book, *The Heathens*, anthropologist William Howells gives a very reasonable explanation of what probably happened in terms of the religious concept of *Tabu*. Many ancient religions (probably most) had the same general custom of holding certain things sacred which were not to be touched by human beings. Among the Hebrews, this idea was very deeply ingrained. Among such tabu objects were: 'dead bodies, mothers after childbirth, most manifestations of sex, warriors, and of course things connected with Jehovah'.[20] Obviously, not all of these things were electrical devices. The unfortunate Uzzah was guilty of tabu-breaking and so he paid the penalty of death. In another instance, whereby the Philistines once got hold of the Ark of the Covenant, they suffered an epidemic as opposed to electrical shock. So the method of Jehovah's vengeance does vary in different instances.

JESUS

Given the general method of reasoning used, one is surprised *not* to find Jesus Christ counted among von Däniken's ancient astronauts. The theory that Jesus was a spaceman has been supported favourably by Jessup, Trench, Drake, and others. Although I do not accept the Jesus-as-spaceman interpretation myself, it is only honest to point out that a better case can be made for it than for most of von Däniken's other examples of alleged extraterrestrials.

In his book, *UFO and the Bible*, the astronomer Jessup addressed his readers as follows:

> . . . I am asking you to give consideration to two or more 'Heavens'. I desire you to accept the possibility that one 'Heaven' is a realm of space in and around the earth-moon binary system, and which is sparsely inhabited by UFO[s] and by one or more races of super-intelligence. I hope that you will be hospitable to the idea that Jesus Christ may have come from this 'heaven' as a representative of a higher or more advanced race . . .[21]

Along similar lines, Trench calls our attention to quotes from the New Testament such as the following, from Mark:

> And then shall they see the Son of man coming in the clouds with great power and glory.
> And then shall he send his angels, and shall gather together his elect from the four winds, from the uttermost part of the earth to the uttermost part of heaven (Mark 13:26–27).[22]

Many churches and cathedrals in Eastern Europe contain sacred paintings called 'icons', depicting the Ascension, Transfiguration, and Second Coming of Christ. Most of the frescoes show lines or rays being emitted from the tail end of the surrounding design, creating a starlike or cometary appearance. Some suggest that perhaps such designs represent various stages of space-flight and that, at the time of the Ascension, Jesus may have been rescued by his fellow spacemen and taken aboard a spaceship (see illus 11). In support of this theory, consider these words found in Matthew 17:5:

> While he yet spake, behold, a bright cloud overshadowed them: and behold a voice out of the cloud, which said, This is my beloved Son, in whom I am well pleased; hear ye him.

Perhaps the most intriguing Biblical passage of all (in the present context) is this one, attributed to Jesus himself:

> And other sheep I have which are not of this fold. Them also I must bring. And they shall hear my voice. And there shall be one fold and one shepherd (John 10:16).

Suppose Jesus was indeed referring to intelligent beings on other worlds. If so, how did *they* come into existence? Von Däniken seems to think that in order for an intelligent race of beings to originate, they need outside help. But if that is the case, how do we account for the 'helpers', and *their* helpers, and so on *ad infinitum*. Plugging in a *Deus ex machina* only begs the question.

Most scientists are inclined to reason that if we can discover how life evolved on Earth, then we should be better able to estimate the chances of the same event happening elsewhere in the universe. And although all of the precise details are not yet known about the process of evolution, there is much information that we do have, and it overwhelmingly points in the direction of a tendency in nature for most organisms to become more and more complex, some reaching a stage that we call 'intelligent'.

SOURCE NOTES
1 W. R. Drake, *Gods or Spacemen?* (Amherst, Wisconsin: Amherst Press, 1964), p22.

2 M. K. Jessup, *UFO and the Bible* (New York: Citadel Press, 1956), pp49–50.

3 Ibid., p98.

4 Erich von Däniken, *Chariots of the Gods?*, trans. Michael Heron (London: Corgi Books, 1971), pp51–2.

5 Ibid., p51.

6 *The Interpreter's Dictionary of the Bible*, in four volumes, ed. George Arthur Buttrick (New York and Nashville: Abingdon Press, 1962), Vol 4, p426.

7 *The Oxford Annotated Bible with the Apocrypha*, Revised Standard Version, ed. Herbert G. May and Bruce M. Metzger (New York: Oxford University Press, 1965), p8.

8 *Chariots of the Gods?*, p52.

9 *The Interpreter's Bible*, in twelve volumes, ed. George Arthur Buttrick (Nashville, TN: Abingdon Press, 1952), Vol 1, p553.

10 *Chariots*, p54.

11 Ibid., p54.

12 Isaac Asimov, *Asimov's Guide to the Bible*, in two volumes (Garden City, NY: Doubleday & Co., 1968), Vol 1, p82.

13 From an article entitled 'Sodom and Gomorrah: the Destruction of the Cities of the Plain', by J. Penrose Harland, in *The Biblical Archaeologist*, Vol 6, No 3, September 1943, pp41–54.

14 *The Oxford Annotated Bible*, p1001.

15 Josef Blumrich, *The Spaceships of Ezekiel* (New York: Bantam Books, 1973), p54.

16 *Chariots*, p55.

17 *The Spaceships of Ezekiel*, p73.

18 *Chariots*, p56.

19 Ibid., pp58–9.

20 William Howells, *The Heathens* (Garden City, NY: Doubleday, 1948), p39.

21 *UFO and the Bible*, p116.

22 Brinsley Le Poer Trench, *The Sky People* (London: Neville Spearman, 1960), p81.

4 THE DAWN OF MAN

Anthropologists generally agree that around ten to fifteen million years ago certain ancestral apes (or 'hominoids') began to encounter dramatic changes in their environment and, by their ability to adapt, they eventually emerged as *Homo sapiens* (the possible misnomer which translates as 'man the wise').

The exact amount of time involved, as well as the exact sequence of changes that took place during this period of development from our extinct ancestors to modern humans, we may never know for sure. Even the much more recent period from 'non-civilised' to 'civilised' (or city-dwelling) man, although now estimated to have taken approximately ten thousand years, may never be totally reconstructed by reason of our inability to return to the past for first-hand verification. So, without a time-machine, archaeology will likely remain an inexact science in that sense.

It is for just this reason that alternative conceptions of the past ages of man should be welcomed. But what is needed along with alternative theories, so they can be properly evaluated, is a renewed awareness of the pitfalls of irrational thought and an active concern for its consequences. Fasle premises, inadequate (and inaccurate) information, logical fallacies (known also as propaganda techniques), closed-mindedness and academic pomposity all contribute to a stifling of the truth – whatever it may be. Von Däniken's 'theory' about early man involves all of these factors and therefore requires careful examination alongside the known facts.

Perhaps the cornerstone of his overall theory is the notion that '. . . unknown beings created human intelligence by a deliberate artificial mutation and that extra-terrestrials ennobled man "in their own image".'[1] Von Däniken says: 'that is why we resemble them – not they us.'[2] I will have more to say about this point shortly. But, first, let us follow some of von Däniken's expanding scenarios beginning with that given in *Chariots of the Gods?*:

Dim as yet undefinable ages ago an unknown space-ship soon found out that the earth had all the prerequisites for intelligent life to develop. Obviously the 'man' of those times was no *homo sapiens*, but something rather different. The spacemen artificially fertilised some female members of this species, put them into a deep sleep, so ancient legends say, and departed. Thousands of years later the space travellers returned and found scattered specimens of the genus *homo sapiens*. They repeated their breeding experiment several times until finally they produced a creature intelligent enough to have the rules of society imparted to it.[3]

Later, writing in *Return to the Stars*, von Däniken concerns himself specifically with the question of the *origin of intelligence* in man. He refers to the notion that '. . . human intelligence seems to have appeared almost overnight'. He seems to define 'intelligence' in terms of: 'The club . . . discovered as a weapon; the bow . . . invented for hunting; fire . . . to serve man's own ends; stone wedges . . . used as tools; the first paintings . . . on the walls of caves'.[4] Also, in *Return to the Stars*, he attempts to date these events: '. . . the first artificial mutation with the genetic code used by the "gods" must have taken place between 40,000 and 20,000 BC. And the second artificial mutation would have occurred in more recent times, between 7,000 and 3,500 BC.'[5]

The founding of humanity takes a new twist in von Däniken's third book, *The Gold of the Gods*. In this version, our astral ancestors are portrayed as 'losers' in a cosmic war said to have taken place 'in the depths of the galaxy'. Escaping from their home planet, with other alien forces in hot pursuit, our ancestral 'gods' set up 'technical stations and transmitters' as a diversion, on what was then the fifth planet from the sun (which is now the fragments making up the asteroid belt between Mars and Jupiter). The pursuers annihilated the decoy planet and returned to home base. The explosion jostled the solar system a bit and the Earth's axis tilted a few degrees causing the Great Flood recounted by Noah in the Bible and in legends from all over the world. After this, the losers decided to lie low for a while so they built a series of subterranean tunnel systems in which to hide. Upon surfacing again, these beings decided to '. . . create intelligence on earth. Using their knowledge of molecular biology, the losers created man *in their image* from already existing monkeys.'[6]

Let us now review some of the preceding points of von Däniken's 'bold new theory' in the light of current anthropological knowledge. Our first point concerns the creation of man in the image of alien beings, which according to von Däniken is why 'we resemble them – not they us'. On the face of it, this may sound like a good argument. But it fails to take into account more than 15 million years of fossil evidence extending from a now-extinct population (whose teeth resembled those of later hominids more than apes), including a whole series of other hominid remains, culminating in modern man. In other words, the human form can be traced back to the *Australopithecines* over five million years ago and perhaps much earlier than that to primates whose features indicate they were probably precursors of our own.

Tool-making man or *Homo habilis* (which translates as 'handy man') goes back over two million years, at which time 'the club as a weapon' was probably invented. The innovation of 'fire to serve man's own ends' can be traced back at least 500,000 years to Peking man (*Homo erectus*), and the 'bow for hunting' probably dates to around 40,000 BC along with 'paintings on the walls of caves'. The main point being that von Däniken's definition of 'intelligence' is difficult to pinpoint in time, especially since the origin and development of man has spanned many millions of years.

In *Return to the Stars*, von Däniken tried to reinforce his notion of the 'sudden' appearances of man by quoting the renowned American anthropologist Loren Eiseley (1908–77).

The statements attributed to Eiseley were as follows:

> To all appearances [man's] brain ultimately underwent a rapid development and it was only then that man finally became distinguished from his other relatives ...
>
> ... we must assume that man only emerged quite recently, because he appeared so explosively. We have every reason to believe that without prejudice to forces that must have shared in the training of the human brain, a stubborn and long-drawn-out battle for existence between several human groups could never have produced such high mental faculties as we find today among all peoples of the earth. Something else, some other educational factor, must have escaped the attention of the evolutionary theoreticians.[7]

Suspecting that Eiseley had at least been quoted out of context (if not misquoted altogether) I wrote to him at the University of Pennsylvania and received the following reply (extracted from a letter dated 22 August 1975), two years before his death:

> Indeed I have heard of the von Däniken books, although I have never bothered to read them through. I do know that I am quoted out of context in one of them. My permission was never sought. I might add that I tried to give in more than one professional paper and in *Darwin's Century* [New York: Doubleday, 1958] an explanation for the comparatively rapid development of the human brain in terms of *natural selection*. I had no intention of making a mystery out of it. The one quotation, of course, predates the recent African discoveries which have greatly extended man's development in time. They were standard matters of discussion among American anthropologists back in the fifties and von Däniken has ignored the fact that the scientific frontier is always changing.
>
> I was dealing, incidentally, with quite another subject revolving around nineteenth century evolutionary philosophy and the quote was never intended to be used in the way von Däniken used it ...
>
> Quite frankly, I believe that these 'occult' approaches to

archaeology appeal to so many people because they represent some intangible attraction in the intellectual atmosphere of our time. It is a fad, in other words, which has been exploited unscrupulously by some publishers and the mass-media as well. I do not believe that it can be combatted very successfully except among a few honest persons. The true believer will shut out any opposing argument and these true believers are to be numbered in the millions. This is what makes these unscrupulous books profitable.

Although difficult to convey in summary form, the explanation Eiseley alluded to in *Darwin's Century* for the emergence of intelligence goes something like this: beginning with a capacity for language (hints of which can be seen in the mammals, particularly the primates) and hence ideation and social intercourse, man may have selected his own values (and nurtured these traits) as opposed to simple adaptation to environmental factors.

Art, morality and abstract thought might have been selected by modern man to improve the quality of life on the intellectual plane. Perhaps the expanded cortex of man gradually introduced him to a new world of thought and ideas that he began to select for himself. There are obvious selective advantages to be learned as opposed to instinctual behaviour. Organisms capable of learning through speech or sign language can adjust their own behaviour more quickly and easily as demanded by a changing environment. Such an advantage would of course tend towards the continued development of the cerebral cortex of the brain wherein man's reasoning powers are thought to reside.

Richard E. Leakey (son of famed anthropologist Louis S. B. and Mary Leakey) and his co-author Roger Lewin (science editor of the *New Scientist* in London) shed more light on the evolution of human intelligence in their new book *People of the Lake.** One of the key points they make is that man's intelligence is not quite so unique — in the animal world - as most of us might think. Tool-using and, more importantly, *tool-making* behaviour among chimpanzees dispels an old notion that man

*Anchor Press/Doubleday, 1978

was unique in that regard. As an example, Leakey and Lewin cite the termite-eating and termite-fishing habits of the chimps at the Gombe Stream Reserve, in Western Tanzania, first observed by Jane Goodall. The chimps break off small tree branches, which they prepare by stripping off the leaves and bark, to use in probing the tunnels made by termites in large clay mounds. The termites bite into the inserted stick which is then quickly withdrawn, and the termites left hanging on are licked off by the chimps. The whole process is much more involved than what my necessarily brief description can convey and demonstrates clearly the 'intelligence' of chimpanzees.

Intelligence in primates is further demonstrated by recent experiments in sign-language communication with chimps and gorillas. Such 'conversations' between humans and apes have revealed a surprising level of comprehension on the part of the primates. Gorillas and chimps seem to understand many *concepts* that, formerly, were thought of as proud possessions of *human* understanding only. But the key to human intelligence is most likely found in the evolution of verbal language. The survival value of verbal language had to be enormous. It is also the kind of development that could have occurred relatively suddenly, ie over a few thousand years.

Some physical anthropologists think that a 'new' anatomical feature of the vocal tract might have developed, between 40,000 to 50,000 years ago, which could have led to more efficient verbal communication over a relatively few number of generations. After all, when one thinks of it, improved communication among human beings is the real key to virtually all progress on this planet. When one considers the fantastic pace at which technological developments have occurred during the past fifty years, it should not seem so amazing that a cultural improvement took place over a period of several thousand years in the lives of our ancestors. Social interaction, enhanced by verbal language, was what allowed them to work together to achieve common goals. But what von Däniken refuses to recognise is that the human way of life, which Leakey and Lewin call 'reciprocal altruism', still took untold millennia to evolve. Traces of its evolution are all too obvious to be denied.

Again, von Däniken's explanation of help from the 'gods', while appealing on the surface, does not take into account an abundance of other ideas being developed by anthropologists. Any serious theory must take into account all relevant knowledge that already exists on a given subject. To ignore most of the existing body of knowledge is one of the standard earmarks of the pseudoscientist.

SOURCE NOTES:

1 Erich von Däniken, *According to the Evidence* (London: Souvenir Press, 1978), p211.
2 Ibid., pv.
3 *Chariots of the Gods?*, pp71–2.
4 Erich von Däniken, *Return to the Stars* (London: Corgi Books, 1972), pp26–7.
5 Ibid., p42.
6 Erich von Däniken, *The Gold of the Gods* (London: Corgi Books, 1974), pp212–13.
7 *Return to the Stars*, p28.

5 'MYSTERIES' OF ANCIENT MEXICO AND SOUTH AMERICA

Von Däniken's usual method of handling archaeological data is as follows: first, he superficially describes some seemingly *mysterious* find, having already plucked it out of context; next, he heightens the 'mystery' by adding erroneous data, from sources unknown; then, he rules out all earthly explanations, usually by mis-stating the true state of our archaeological knowledge, leaving only one possible answer – ancient astronauts.

What appears to be his favourite technique is what logicians call the *argumentum ad ignorantiam*, or 'the appeal to ignorance', which usually takes the form: 'since X cannot be disproved, then it is probably true.' The *argumentum ad ignorantiam* is related to the fallacy of wishful thinking. If one wants badly enough for something to be true, in spite of any real evidence, it becomes easy to ignore the facts. The statement: 'people believe what they want to believe' has become a cliché, and yet, how often do we realise the sad truth it conveys?

The burden of proof for any claim must logically rest with the *claimant*. Any time the person making a claim 'out of the blue', so to speak, tries to escape backing it up by shifting the burden of proof to his audience, he (or she) is committing the *argumentum ad ignorantiam* fallacy.

Another frequent manoeuvre of von Däniken is to state conclusions (again, those that his audience wants to hear) that do not follow from his premises. The form of the false argument used here is the *non sequitur*, which translates: 'it does not follow'. Von Däniken derides this kind of false reasoning, while committing it himself all too frequently. While mocking scientists of five hundred years ago, he quotes one of them as asserting: 'Nowhere in the Bible . . . does it say that the earth revolves around the sun! Consequently every such assertion is the work of the devil!'[1] Then, a few pages later, he uses the same form of argument to try to establish one of his own conclusions. He says, ' "Giants" haunt the pages of almost all ancient books. So they must have existed.'[2] The fallacy is all too obvious. Furthermore, there is no legitimate archaeological evidence to support such claims. Logic and scientific method work hand-in-hand, and von Däniken seems not to have grasped either one.

In the pages that follow, we shall examine von Däniken's 'proof' of ancient astronauts as it exists in the form of alleged archaeological evidence. We will subject each example to the normal rules of evidence and logical thinking. As I have stated in the Preface to this book, I am not objecting to the basic idea that it is *possible* that intelligent beings from another planet *could have* visited Earth in ancient times. But, I do intend to demonstrate that the archaeological 'wonders' that von Däniken has selected and offered as 'proof' of Space-Gods are largely a collection of interesting finds, superficially described and taken out of context; and, perhaps the most serious deficiency of von Däniken's whole reasoning process: the omission of highly relevant, key information that, if known, would cast an entirely different light on the subject at hand. What follows are some of the most famous examples from von Däniken's showcase of 'proofs' to illustrate what I mean.

THE PALENQUE 'ASTRONAUT'

In the ancient Maya city of Palenque (on the Yucatan Peninsula, in the state of Chiapas, Mexico) stands a seventy-foot-high limestone pyramid called the Temple of the Inscriptions (see illus 12). Until 1949, the interior of the structure had remained unexplored. But when the Mexican archaeologist Alberto Ruz Lhuillier noticed finger-holes in one of the large floor slabs, he raised the stone and discovered a hidden stairway that had been deliberately

54

filled in, centuries ago, with stone and rubble and clay. After four years of clearing away the blockage, Ruz and his workers had descended sixty-five feet into the pyramid, where he came upon a secret tomb. Little did Ruz know that twenty years later this discovery would be used as one of the 'proofs' of the existence of ancient astronauts.*

What has attracted the attention of ancient-astronaut fans everywhere is the stone carving that decorates the tomb lid. Von Däniken describes it this way:

On the slab [covering the tomb is] a wonderful chiseled relief. In my eyes, you can see a kind of frame. In the centre of that frame is a man sitting, bending forward. He has a mask on his nose, he uses his two hands to manipulate some controls, and the heel of his left foot is on a kind of pedal with different adjustments. The rear portion is separated from him; he is sitting on a complicated chair, and outside of this whole frame you see a little flame-like exhaust.†

Could it be that the Palenque tomb lid (see illus 13) actually depicts a man piloting a rocket? Undeniably, if you look at the carving a certain way such a scene can be imagined. The notion becomes less plausible, however, once the various elements that make up the overall design are examined separately, in detail (see illus 14).

The 'rocket' is actually a composite art form, incorporating the design of a cross, a two-headed serpent, and some large corn leaves. Furthermore, the 'oxygen mask' is an ornament that does not connect with the nostrils, but rather seems to touch the tip of the man's nose; the 'controls' are not really associated with the hands, but are elements from a profile view of the Maya Sun

*The 'spaceman' interpretation was suggested originally by the French authors Guy Tarade and Andre Millou and published in the October 1966 issue of the Italian magazine *Clypeus*.

†Quoted from a transcript of *The Lou Gordon Program* (WKBD-TV), videotaped in Detroit, Michigan on 27 February 1976, on which the writer appeared with von Däniken in a televised debate.

God in the background; the 'pedal' operated by the 'astronaut's' foot is a sea shell (a Maya symbol associated with death); and the 'rocket's exhaust' is very likely the roots of the sacred maize tree (the cross), which is symbolic of the life-sustaining corn plant. The whole scene is a religious illustration, not a technological one, and is well understood within the proper context of Maya religious art. (The sculpture is actually a tribute to the Maya King Lord-Shield Pacal, who died in AD 693.)

CARACOL OBSERVATORY

In *Chariots of the Gods?* von Däniken speaks of the Caracol Observatory at Chichén Itzá, Yucatan, as if it were an example of modern-day technology. The bottom portion of the structure does indeed resemble the circular building at Mount Palomar, but here is where the superficial resemblance ends. There is no 'dome' or 'hatches' as von Däniken claims, nor does the building contain a sophisticated reflector telescope as does the observatory at Palomar. He also asks: 'How did the Mayas know about Uranus and Neptune?' The answer is: *they didn't*. Where von Däniken got this idea, I do not know.

As usual, our god-seeker tries to make something out of nothing, as far as evidence for ancient astronauts is concerned. The truth about the Maya observatory is as follows: it is of limestone construction and was built probably about AD 1000. There are four doorways in the building which are aligned with the cardinal points. At the top of a spiral stairway, three windows are found still intact. Through them, Maya astronomer-priests could observe sunset, moonset and the position of Venus at the equinox and solstice points, marking the four seasons.

It was, of course, an admirable achievement for the early Mesoamericans, but not one necessitating extraterrestrial contact. It is quite obviously very crude in comparison with our modern-day observatories, utilising powerful telescopes, atomic clocks and electronic computers.

CENOTES AT CHICHÉN ITZÁ

Before leaving Chichén Itzá, we should take note of the absurdities von Däniken utters about the Sacred Wells located there. First of all, he has the idea that the two wells at Chichén (called 'Well of Sacrifice' and 'Xtoloc Well') are exactly alike, with the same measurements. He also implies that archaeologists have kept one of the wells a secret to hide the mystery of the matching pair. Speaking of the most famous Sacred Well, von Däniken asks: 'How did this water-hole come into being?'[3] His own explanation is that both wells resulted from the impact of meteorites.

The wells, called 'cenotes', are actually sinkholes, roughly similar to others found in northern Yucatan where limestone is abundant. Geologists think they are formed by water soaking into soft spots in sub-crystalline limestone. The water dissolves the soft rock and forms hollow pockets. Eventually, the roofs of these naturally formed caverns collapse and a round cenote is formed.

In times of unusual hardship, such as droughts or epidemics, the Mayan priests would offer human sacrifices and precious ornaments to the gods by tossing them into the Sacred Well. Archaeologists have since recovered thousands of artifacts and countless human skeletons by dredging the two wells. As to the alleged secrecy of the second well, I had no trouble finding it marked prominently on a full colour map in the *National Geographic** published seven years prior to *Chariots of the Gods?*

OLMECS

Centuries before the Maya, a truly mysterious tribe, which we call today the 'Olmecs' (meaning 'rubber people', named for the area which is rich in rubber trees), lived in the region which today forms the Mexican states of Veracruz and Tabasco. These people are believed by archaeologists to have been the mother

*Vol 120, No 4, October 1961, p545.

cultures of the Maya, Aztecs, and Toltecs. Von Däniken calls our attention to the amazing Olmec sculptures – the 'beautifully helmeted giant skulls' – which he thinks are surely reminiscent of astronaut-gear.[4]

The colossal heads, which were carved from basalt, are truly remarkable. Their size ranges between five and ten feet in height and they weigh from 15 to 30 tons. The head coverings depicted on the carvings are, no doubt, helmets. In fact, they are similar to those worn by Maya ballplayers. The football-style helmet was a part of the attire used in a game similar to basketball in which a rubber ball was thrown through a hoop carved from stone or wood. These ball games were serious business in which large bets were made. One could win or lose gold, turquoise, slaves, cornfields, or houses. On occasion, the players' own lives were at stake. No wonder, then, the heroes of these games were idolised, and perhaps even depicted in the Olmec sculptures.

TIAHUANACO

According to von Däniken, the real cradle of mankind was Tiahuanaco, Bolivia. In *Return to the Stars* he says: 'Traditional legends and existing stone drawings tell us that the "gods" met at Tiahuanaco before man was even created. In the language of our space age that means that unknown astronauts constructed their first base on the Bolivian plateau.' And 'when the Spanish *conquistadores* asked the natives about the builders of Tiahuanaco in the 1530s, they could give no information about them. They referred the Spaniards to the sagas, according to which Tiahuanaco was the place where the gods had created men.'[5] He goes on to tell how mysterious the place is and that (as usual) archaeologists know practically nothing about it. And, here again, von Däniken tries to divert the reader away from the abundant archaeologcal knowledge that does truly exist.

The Tiahuanaco culture can be traced back to cave dwellers who utilised stone and bone tools, at around 9000 BC, and a sequence of occupation established up through historic times. The early migrants were probably nomadic hunters, fishermen and gatherers who crossed the Isthmus of Panama and eventually migrated into South America. Eventually, these people domesticated the plants and animals already native to this region, and began to build ceremonial centres (probably around 1800 BC). Archaeologists have suggested a chronology for the city of Tiahuanaco itself lasting from about 200 BC to AD1200.

The stonemasonry here is some of the best in the Andes and has inspired a rash of far-fetched notions from von Däniken. He cannot imagine how such a primitive culture as the Tiahuanaco Empire could be responsible for the 'technological' achievements there. From sources unknown, von Däniken cites the following legend: 'It tells of a golden space-ship that came from the stars; in it came a woman, whose name was Oryana, to fulfil the task of becoming the Great Mother of the earth. Oryana had only four fingers, which were webbed. Great Mother Oryana gave birth to seventy earth children, then she returned to the stars.'[6] Strangely enough, no archaeologist seems to know of this legend and the only other reference to it I could find was in Robert Charroux's *One Hundred Thousand Years of Man's Unknown History*, another work of pseudoscience just as unreliable as the books of von Däniken.

I suspect that another legend, associated with Tiahuanaco, would serve his purpose just as well – that the city '. . . was built in a single night, after the flood, by unknown giants. But they disregarded a prophecy of the coming of the sun and were annihilated by its rays, and their palaces were reduced to ashes . . .'[7] Could they have been blasted off the face of the Earth in a big shoot-em-up with ray guns?

First of all, it was common for later civilisations to attribute colossal stoneworks, left behind by their unknown ancestors, to the work of 'giants', for lack of a better explanation. There is no doubt that civilisation has developed in cycles rather than one unbroken chain from primitive to complex. Obviously, progress is enhanced once communication links are established between different parts of the world so that knowledge can be shared and discoveries built one on top of the other. This kind of synthesised knowledge is our modern way of life. But the peoples of antiquity had to be even more ingenious than us. Their life and livelihood depended upon their ability to figure out things for themselves. We certainly don't give them very much credit if we attribute our ancestors' greatest accomplishments to the whimsical visits of spacemen.

THE NAZCA 'SPACEPORT'

It is possible, if not likely, that the Tiahuanaco culture gave birth (as they migrated north) to another 'lost civilisation' – the Ica-Nazca of south-western Peru. The Nazcas left behind a tradition of fine weaving, beautifully decorated ceramics, and possibly the remnants of an astronomical calendar.

About 250 miles south-east of Lima, between the towns of Nazca and Palpa, lies a barren plateau covering 200 square miles that, when observed from the air, reveals etchings of over 13,000 lines, more than 100 spirals, trapezoids and triangles, and nearly 800 huge animals. Most of the lines radiate from several star-like centres and extend for miles. These markings were probably constructed (over a period of several hundred years) some time between 400 BC and AD 900.

In his book *Return to the Stars*, von Däniken tells us his theory: 'At some time in the past, unknown intelligences landed on the uninhabited plain near the present-day town of Nazca and built an improvised airfield for their spacecraft which were to operate in the vicinity of the earth.'[8]

In *The Space-Gods Revealed*, I gave reasons why the lines were probably *not* ancient landing strips, namely that: (1) there simply would be no need for a runway, several miles long, to accommodate a space vehicle that should be capable of a vertical landing, and (2) the soft, sandy soil would not be a suitable surface for any kind of heavy vehicle to land on.

More recently, von Däniken has modified his Nazca spaceport theory as follows: 'The argument that the extraterrestrials would not need runways because they would take-off and land vertically is obsolete for two reasons. Firstly, I have not claimed that extraterrestrials had built the tracks at Nazca. I have only said that these tracks were the result of some sort of cargo-cult of the

60

natives there. And secondly, didn't NASA build a huge runway for spaceships in California? For the space-shuttle?'[9]

As can be seen by the above quote from *Return to the Stars*, von Däniken did indeed say that the extraterrestrials '. . . built an improvised airfield . . .' Furthermore, many of the Nazca 'runways' run right into hills, ridges and the sides of mountains. Wouldn't that cause a few problems for a vehicle like the space-shuttle?

Another version of the spaceport theory maintains that the exhaust from hovering spacecraft was responsible for blowing away the sand and thus creating the lines. Again, a nice try, but this idea would seem to prove just the opposite of what its proponents intend. It is not the lightweight soil that was removed to create the lines, but rather the heavier rocks, that are actually stacked in linear piles all along the borders of the lines and figures.

What then, could have been the purpose of such an enormous array of lines, shapes, and animal figures created more than a thousand years ago?

The first systematic study of the Nazca markings came in 1939 (twelve years after their actual discovery in modern times),* when Professor Paul Kosok of Long Island University first mapped and photographed them from the air. His most significant finding came, however, while he was standing on the ground gazing down one of the lines towards the setting sun on 22 June 1941. This happened to be the day of the winter solstice in the Southern Hemisphere; and the apparent alignment gave Kosok the startling idea: perhaps the lines represented 'the largest astronomy book in the world'.[10] He later confirmed more than a dozen such alignments, some for the solstices and others for the equinoxes, indicating that the Nazca 'landing field' very likely comprised a gigantic astronomical calendar and observatory. It has been found also that several of the large animal drawings have solstice lines associated with them. After all, how would the Nazcans be able to recognise which lines were which, if they had

---

*The actual discovery of the Nazca markings (in 1927) is credited to Toribio Mexta Xesspe, a member of a Peruvian aerial survey team.

not devised some reference system by which to find them later?

Von Däniken and some others have rejected the Nazca calendar theory because, they say, not *all* of the lines have been shown to be astronomically oriented. We must realise, however, that this does not *erase* the fact of the many solstice lines that *have* been discovered. These also 'happen' to be special lines marked prominently by certain bird, spider, and animal figures.

The fact that *most* of the lines on the Nazca plain radiate from central *mounds* also appears significant, and fits logically the theory that they were used as sight-lines. It would also seem to make more sense if the sun and moon were the referents used for such a timekeeping system rather than stars, since the lines would, of course, be more difficult to see in the dark. Detractors of the calendar theory also overlook the possibility of other *kinds* of alignments, such as how the shadows of certain hills and ridges marked by the lines, might also have been used in ways we do not yet (and may never) understand.

But the question is still asked: why would the ancient Nazcans go to such trouble to construct these markings (and especially the drawings of animals) that are recognisable only from the air? (See illus 15–18.) In fact, the most ideal vantage point for viewing them is *not* from hundreds of miles up, where one might expect to find an orbiting satellite or a spaceship, but rather, at a point in mid-air, about 600 feet above the plain. How then, could the early Peruvians have seen and appreciated their work without the advantage of something like an early-model helicopter?

According to a theory recently tested by the Florida-based International Explorers Society, the 'chariots of the gods' that sailed over Nazca might well have been early-model smoke balloons, piloted not by alien beings but by ancient man himself. In a recent book entitled *NAZCA: Journey to the Sun*,* IES member Jim Woodman presents an impressive array of evidence to support his contention that the early Peruvians knew the secret of lighter-than-air flight long before the first hot-air balloons had ever been flown in Europe.

For example, all along the Nazca plain are thousands of ancient

*Simon & Schuster, 1977.

grave-sites containing finely woven textiles (perfectly suited for balloon envelopes), braided rope (another item useful in balloon-making), and ceramic pottery. On one of the clay pots is a picture that resembles a hot-air bag complete with tie ropes (see illus 19). There is also the little known fact that, even in modern times the Europeans were not the first to make manned balloon flights. In the city plaza of Santos, Brazil, stands a monument to 'the flying man' Bartolomeu de Gusmão, who reportedly made his first flight in October 1709.

On 28 November 1975, author Jim Woodman and the noted balloonist Julian Nott tested their theory by flying over the Nazca plain in a reconstructed version of a primitive smoke balloon (see illus 20) that was made exclusively of materials which the ancient Nazcans were known to possess.

It was a remarkable example of archaeology-by-experiment, in which an ancient possibility had been demonstrated without having to resort to the Space-God theory.

TRIDENT OF PISCO BAY

An interesting sidelight to the Nazca spaceport theory is the alleged connection with another 'beacon to the gods' – the 'Candelabra of the Andes' or Trident of Pisco Bay (see illus 21, 22). It is declared a total mystery by von Däniken, unless . . . of course, you accept his alien-visitation theory. 'To be honest,' he says, in *Chariots of the Gods?*, 'we must admit that we are groping in the dark when we try to explain it. It cannot be meaningfully included in existing dogmas, which does not mean to say that there may not be some trick by which scholars could conjure this phenomenon too into the great mosaic of accepted archaeological thinking.'[11]

In *Return to the Stars*, he goes a bit further. The trident symbol, he says, is 820 feet high but cannot be seen well from the sea. And since it points 'heavenwards' it must have been meant as some kind of signal to aerial vehicles. He also claims that the giant 'candlestick', or trident consists of 'snow-white phosphorescent blocks that are as hard as granite'.[12] He states his own theory as follows: 'Nazca is 100 miles as the crow flies from Pisco. Suddenly I had a brainwave. Was there some connection between the trident in the Bay of Pisco, the figures on the plain of Nazca and the ruins on the plateau of Tiahuanaco? Apart from a very slight deviation, they are joined by a straight line drawn on the map.'[13] Let us now look at the facts.

In reality the trident symbol is 494 feet in height, somewhat smaller than von Däniken claims, but can easily be seen at a distance of 20 kilometres out at sea. In fact, it serves as an excellent marker for fishermen so that they can easily find their way back into port. In other words, the trident does not face just 'heavenwards', but is actually situated at an angle of 42°, on the face of a cliff overlooking Pisco Bay (also known as the Bay of Paracas, because of the Paracas Peninsula).

The information that the trident is constructed from 'phosphorescent blocks . . . as hard as granite' is also in error. It is in fact carved into a white, stony salt crust that lies below four feet of soft sand. The white glow of the sign is from pure salt, which gleams in the sunlight.

Another error is that old line about the trident symbol pointing to Nazca. It is in fact several degrees off; and any astronaut following it (if for some reason he lacked more sophisticated navigational methods) would miss Nazca by about 150 miles.

Now, to explain the meaning of the giant symbol. It just happens that this sign is located on the locally famous 'Red Hill' (more properly called Cerro Colorado), at the site of the celebrated cemetery of Paracas, one of the two largest prehistoric cemeteries in Peru. Hundreds of mummified bodies have been excavated from one of the tens of caverns that are located there; and even today, one can find a scattering of human bones left by grave robbers, creating a rather macabre sight.

The three crosses making up the trident actually represent the 'tree of life' (and death), common to many ancient religions, particularly in Mexico and South America. The universal symbol is quite simply related to life and death, and denotes here a burial ground just as the cross of Jesus is displayed at Christian cemeteries today. Here is symbolised the triad of the sun, moon, and Earth. Man is also seen triadically, by the Quichuas

3

1. The author with Dr Clifford Wilson in Phoenix, Arizona on 18 February 1978. *Photo by David Scott.*

2. Erich von Däniken.

3. Morris K. Jessup.

4

4. Southern bay of the Dead Sea. Drawing from *The Book of the Prophet Ezekiel*, by C.H. Toy (New York: Dodd, Mead & Co., 1899).

5. Reconstruction of Cherub-Chariot. Drawing from *The Book of the Prophet Ezekiel*.

6. Position of wheels of the Cherub-Chariot. Drawing from *The Book of the Prophet Ezekiel*.

7-10: Assyrian Cherubic Figures, from *The Book of the Prophet Ezekiel:*

7. Eagle-Headed Deity.

8. Four-winged Deity.

9. Human-headed Colossal Lion.

10. Human-headed, Winged Bull-Deity.

11. Could this be a space-helmet on the head of Jesus?

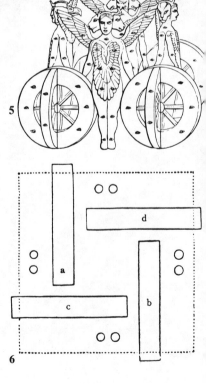

8

11

12

12. The Temple of the Inscriptions, Palenque, Mexico. *Photo by Merle Greene Robertson.*

13. Pacal's tomb lid, depicting the deceased ruler on his throne as he is suspended between the worlds of the living and the dead. At the upper centre of the picture is the cross, symbolising the sacred maize tree (giver of life) and below him, the face of the Earth Monster about to receive his physical remains. At the top of the cross sits the Quetzal bird, herald of the dawn, and over the arms of the cross is draped a two-headed serpent. *Photo and rubbing by Merle Greene Robertson.*

14. From the Temple of the Cross, Palenque. Note similarities to 'rocket' on Pacal's tomb lid. Drawing by Linda Schele. *By permission of the Pre-Columban Art Research Centre, Palenque, Mexico.*

15. Spider depicted on the Nazca plain. The prominent line running through the figure is a solstice line. *Photo courtesy of the International Explorers Society.*

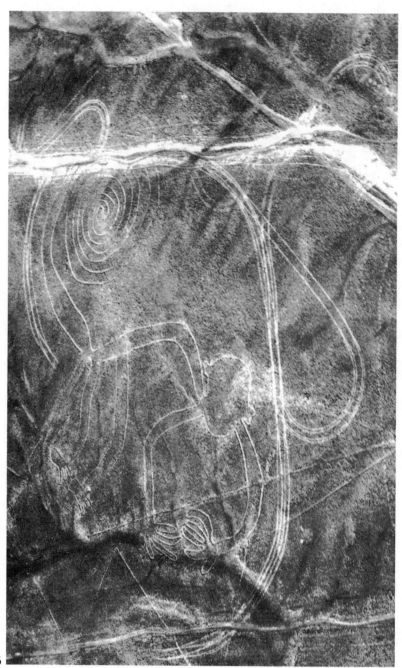

17

16. Giant Monkey on the Nazca Plain. Note, also, tire tracks of off-the-road vehicles which give approximate scale. *Photo courtesy of the International Explorers Society.*

17. The Nazca 'spaceport'. *Photo courtesy of the International Explorers Society.*

19

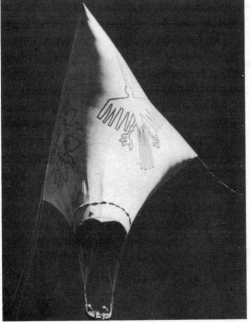

20

18. Giant Condor on the Nazca Plain. Note that the line 'drawn' parallel with the wings is a solstice line. *Photo courtesy of the International Explorers Society.*

19. Pottery shard showing representation of balloon with tie ropes. *Photo courtesy of the International Explorers Society.*

20. Condor I in flight. *Photo courtesy of the International Explorers Society.*

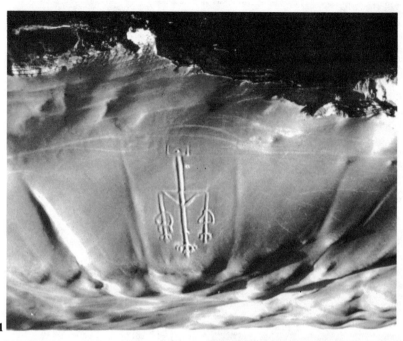

21

21. The Trident of Pisco Bay in Peru. *Photo courtesy of the International Explorers Society.*

22. The Pisco Trident, a close-up view. *Photo courtesy of the International Explorers Society.*

23. Idol shown on cover of von Däniken's book *The Gold of the Gods.* This photo of the same idol was taken by archaeologist Pino Turolla, in 1969, during his own investigation of the Crespi collection. The idol is actually made of brass, not gold. *Photo courtesy of Pino Turolla.*

24. Archaeologist Pino Turolla, in this photo, taken in 1969, is shown looking at Father Crespi's 'fabulous collection'. The dome in the lower-right foreground appears in von Däniken's book *(The Gold of the Gods,* Corgi paperback edition, p15) giving the impression that it is dwelling-size, and the claim is made that it is 'probably the very first dome ever built'. Von Däniken also claims in his book that he photographed it inside the Ecuadorian cave! *Photo courtesy of Pino Turolla.*

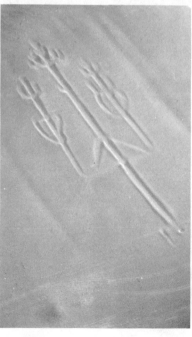

22

23

24

25

25. Archaeologist Pino Turolla, photographed in 1969, holding the 'gold steel . . . showpiece' of the Crespi collection, according to von Däniken (see *the Gold of the Gods,* p54). *Photo courtesy of Pino Turolla.*

26. Dr Louse M. Jilek-Aall, MD, with Padre Crespi. Photo taken in the Church of Maria Auziliadora in Cuenca, Ecuador (in 1971), by Dr Wolfgang G. Jilek, MD.

27. Some of the 'fabulous gold artifacts' (really brass) of the Crespi collection being investigated by Dr Wolfgang Jilek. *Photo by Dr Louise Jilek-Aall.*

Indians of Bolivia, as sensitivity, intelligence and affection; or in other words, as sensory feelings, thought and the heart. The sacred tree also symbolises man with his roots in the earth, and as a collective or social being, with several individuals tied to a common centre. The trident symbol, therefore, stands for the mysteries of life and death, marking sacred grounds for the naturalistic gods of Earth and ancient people of Peru – not giants from Mars or naked ladies from Venus.*

CAVES OF GOLD

The most controversial of von Däniken's books was *The Gold of the Gods*, in which he claimed to have seen the 'Golden Zoo' (a fantastic collection of animal statues made of solid gold) and 'Metal Library' (two or three thousand gold-leaf plaques embossed with an unknown script) in a subterranean tunnel system 800 feet beneath Ecuador and Peru. In this, von Däniken's third book, we find a collection of photographs, purportedly of gold treasures, which had been entrusted to one Padre Carlo Crespi of the Church of Maria Auxiliadora at Cuenca in Ecuador.

What is the significance of this find? Quoting a South American professor, Miloslav Stingl, von Däniken publishes this statement: 'If these pictures are genuine, and everything indicates that they are, because no one makes forgeries in gold, at any rate not on such a large scale, this is the biggest archaeological sensation since the discovery of Troy.'[14] (More about Father Crespi and the 'artifacts' later.)

In March 1972, von Däniken met an Argentine adventurer-explorer Juan Moricz, who, according to the account given in *The Gold of the Gods*, was the discoverer of the caves. It is also stated by von Däniken that Moricz took him on a personal tour through the mysterious underworld. In fact, von Däniken begins his book by saying: 'To me this is the most incredible, fantastic story of the century. It could easily have come straight from the realms of science fiction if I had not seen and photographed the incredible truth in person.'[15] But when the German news magazine

*Referring to the 'Orejona legend'.

65

Der Spiegel dispatched a reporter to interview Juan Moricz in Ecuador, Moricz said: 'Däniken has never been in the caves – unless it was in a flying saucer. If he claims to have seen the library and other things himself then that's a lie.'[16] According to Moricz, during the first week in March 1972, von Däniken invited him over for a meal at the Atahualpa Hotel in Guayaquil, Ecuador. Here they began discussing the cave story, one detail leading to another. Moricz said: 'I told him everything. For hours, for days, he squeezed it out of me.'[17] This information was later passed on to von Däniken's readers as his own experiences. What, apparently, von Däniken did not know was that the cave story was not even original with Moricz. It is said that the legend can be traced back more than thirty years to a deranged army captain named Jaramillo.

There was a cave expedition, led by Moricz, in 1969. He was accompanied by fourteen persons including a local Indian chief, Nayambi, of the Coangos tribe. Although they did find an artificially carved stone archway and some walls of carved granite blocks, there were no gold treasures not any evidence of our alleged astral ancestors.

Count Pino G. Turolla of Istria (now a resident of Miami Beach, Florida) paid a visit to Padre Crespi in 1969 and took many photographs of the good father's collection (see illus 23–27). Turolla found that the 'priceless artifacts' were neither ancient nor made of gold, but were contemporary brass trinkets, similar to those commonly sold to tourists in Cuenca (see illus 22–26).[18] Father Crespi obtains the pieces from local Indians who trade him their handiwork for clothes or small sums of money.[19]

In further support of Turolla's testimony, two Canadian psychiatrists, Drs Wolfgang and Louise Jilek, reported their findings after a trip to Ecuador in 1971. The following 'letter to the editor' was published by *The Skeptical Inquirer* (formerly called *The Zetetic*) (the journal of the Committee for the Scientific Investigation of Claims of the Paranormal) in their Spring/ Summer 1978 issue.

CRESPI'S 'TREASURES'

In 1971, we had the opportunity, before Erich von Däniken,

to inspect the alleged gold and silver treasures he later claimed to be of extraterrestrial provenance. This opportunity came when getting acquainted with Father Carlo Crespi of Santa Maria Auxiliadora church in Cuenca, Ecuador, who already at that time was in his eighties, impaired of vision and hearing. Formerly a serious archaeologist, Father Crespi had with advancing age become a victim of his well-known scientific hypotheses of Egyptian origin of pre-Columbian art. He had purchased from local entrepreneurs the rather monstrous assortment of giant paddles, lyres, sarcophagi, bass fiddles, folio volumes, etc, allegedly *puro oro y plata* and inscribed with hieroglyphs, also featuring crude 'African' images of elephants and 'pyramids' as 'proof' of their trans-atlantic origin. Obviously, local craftsmen had taken advantage of the aging padre's pet theories and funds. They were, however, not the only ones to take advantage of Father Crespi, who no doubt was easily persuaded by von Däniken to antedate the origin of his collection so as to further promote this author's 'evidence' of galactic visitors spawning culture down here on our planet. It is difficult to assume that von Däniken was so naïve as to really believe this collection of brass and sheet-metal artifacts to be made of gold and silver, and the clumsy folk-images of 'hieroglyphs', snakes, animals, and cheerfully smiling 'gods' to represent code-writings by extraterrestrial intelligences, pre-historic fauna, and likenesses of galactic space-travellers. We took photographs of some of these trea-sures, and we also have a souvenir sample which the good Father gave us to have examined in Canada. It sadly confirmed our immediate impression of contemporary folk art using brass, not gold, as material base.

As psychiatrists and anthropologists we may be permitted the comment that the real significance of von Däniken's enormous literary success, also with intellectual readers, has little to do with scientific, or even popular scientific, interests of the public. Rather it has to do with modern man's *anomie* and alienation and his hope that, although the old Gods are dead, some *deus ex machina* may soon step out of an extra-terrestrial spaceship and with his supra-human intelligence and technological power lead us out of the mess we created on this planet. Von Däniken must be credited with catering to this pseudo-religious need of industrialised man who looks up to the skies for instant socio-politico-economical salvation by fabulously smart and powerful little green men arriving in UFOs from outer space, just as in von Däniken's clever movie the cargo-cultists on a South Sea island gaze up to the clouds expecting the cargo planes to soon deliver the goodies.

Wolfgang G. Jilek, MD
Louise M. Jilek-Aall, MD
Tsawwassen Delta
6 January 1978   British Columbia, Canada

SOURCE NOTES

1 *Chariots of the Gods?* p46.
2 Ibid., p52.
3 Ibid., p126.
4 Ibid., p117.
5 *Return to the Stars*, pp52–3.
6 *Chariots*, p37.
7 *The World's Last Mysteries* (Pleasantville, New York: Reader's Digest, 1976), p133.
8 *Return to the Stars*, p118.
9 *Second Look*, January 1979, p13; article entitled: 'Why Do Critics Ignore The Positive Arguments For Ancient Astronauts?' by Erich von Däniken.
10 Paul Kosok and Maria Reiche, 'The Mysterious Markings of Nazca', *Natural History* May 1947, p203.
11 *Chariots*, p33.
12 *Return to the Stars*, p114.
13 Ibid., p119.
14 Ibid., p46.
15 Ibid., p1.
16 *Der Spiegel*, No12/1973 (19 March 1973), p156.
17 Ibid., p156.
18 *Der Spiegel*, No36/1972 (28 August 1972), p120.
19 John Keasler, 'Von Däniken's "Golden Gods": Great Find or Great Fraud?' *Miami News*, 17 October 1973.

Next, we visit one of the loneliest places on Earth. Its prehistoric inhabitants called it *Te Pito o te Henua* or The Navel of the World (the modern natives call it Rapa Nui); but because the Dutch Admiral Jacob Roggeveen discovered this tiny dot of land in the South Pacific on Easter Sunday 1722, it has since been known to the rest of the world as Easter Island (see illus 28). Of all the inhabited places on Earth, Easter Island is one of the most isolated by the sea. Its location is 2,300 miles due east of Chile (the country to which it belongs) and 1,300 miles west of Pitcairn Island (famed refugee of the *Bounty* mutineers). Partly because of such extreme isolation, its earliest inhabitants have been regarded as one of the most curious cultures of the ancient world. They had their own system of picture writing (unlike any other language in the world), a fairly sophisticated political and religious structure, and a tradition of stone working that resulted in over 600 colossal heads (up to 32 feet in height and weighing up to 82 metric tons) carved from volcanic stone (see illus 29, 30).

The statues have inspired a long tradition of pseudoscientific speculation, culminating today in von Däniken's Space-God theory. Pseudo-archaeologists have 'identified' the Easter Island culture as the remnants of a sunken Pacific continent, such as the Lost Continent of Mu, or even as migrants of the much more distant and equally hypothetical 'Lost World' of Atlantis. Among legitimate archaeologists, there is little doubt that Easter Island was first populated by Polynesians from the Marquesas Islands, to the north-west, probably about the first century AD. The ancient seafarers of Polynesia are known to have been excellent navigators and to have built huge double-hulled voyaging canoes that could carry heavy loads of food, water, and domesticated plants and animals, with which to start a new colony.

This theory (which is backed by abundant evidence) is rejected by von Däniken, who implies that the giant stone statues must be modelled after space-beings since (he claims) they do not resemble any people on Earth. In his fourth book, *In Search of Ancient Gods*, he says:

> If Polynesians were the creators of the statues, no one has yet explained where they got the models for the shapes and expressions of the statues from. No member of any known Polynesian tribe has such characteristics: long, straight noses, tight-lipped mouths, sunken eyes and low foreheads. Nor can anyone say who is actually supposed to be depicted.[1]

Actually, the main stylistic features of the stone faces do resemble the predominant facial features of the Easter Island natives – and strikingly so – despite von Däniken's false statements to the contrary.*

Some of his other assertions concerning the 'mysteries' of Easter Island are as follows:

> The first European seafarers who landed on Easter Island at the beginning of the eighteenth century could scarcely believe their eyes . . . they saw hundreds of colossal statues, which lay scattered about all over the island. Whole mountain massifs had been transformed, steel-hard volcanic rock had been cut through like butter and 10,000 tons of massive rocks lay in places where they could not have been dressed.[2]

No trees grow on the island, which is a tiny speck of volcanic

*A very nice comparison is shown in an illustrated article entitled 'Easter Island and Its Mysterious Monuments' by H. La Fay and T. J. Abercrombie in the *National Geographic*, Vol 121, No 1, January 1962, p99.

stone. The usual explanation, that the stone giants were moved to their present sites on wooden rollers, is not feasible in this case, either. In addition, the island can scarcely have provided food for more than 2,000 inhabitants.

Then who cut the statues out of the rock, who carved them and transported them to their sites? How were they moved across country for miles without rollers?

Even if people with lively imaginations have tried to picture the Egyptian pyramids being built by a vast army of workers using the 'heave-ho' method, a similar method would have been impossible on Easter Island for lack of manpower.

No, 2,000 men alone could not have made the gigantic statues. And a larger population is inconceivable on Easter Island. Then who did this work? And how did they manage it?[3]

Von Däniken gave a revised version of his own theory (which differs slightly from what is given in his earlier books) on the *Lou Gordon Program* (WKBD-TV, Detroit, Michigan) broadcast in March of 1976:

Somebody had an unknown tool to us – I guess from visitors from outer space – for some reason. We cannot go into detail because of time. [Details have never been given, and I am still eagerly awaiting them.] And with these tools he chiselled, or he burned, or he I-don't-know-what, very easy, like making a figurine into butter with a hot knife today.

One day the tool was broken or the energy was out or the men who knew how to handle it died out. At this moment still two hundred unfinished statues were left in the crater. They are still there today.

It is difficult to imagine how anyone could arrive at such a gross misrepresentation of the facts as von Däniken's, concerning the archaeology of Easter Island. In fact, it serves as a classic example of how facts are ignored or distorted to serve the purpose desired by the pseudoscientist. There is a long history of fanatics who have doctored their data to fit their own preconceived 'theories'. One explorer fudged his drawings of Maya ruins to support his view that the Maya were of Phoenician or Roman descent. Another was caught filing down a stone on the Great Pyramid (in Egypt) so that his formula would come out right! Von Däniken clearly fits this pattern. In his missionary zeal to promote an idea (which is not so outlandish *in itself* were it not for lack of evidence) he fudges with the data so that it indicates what he wants. He confirmed this point in an interview for *Playboy* magazine when he said: 'It's true that I accept what I like and reject what I don't like, but every theologian does the same. Everyone accepts what he needs for his theory, and to the rest he says, "That's a misunderstanding".'[4] That may be true for other pseudoscience writers but legitimate scholars don't usually operate that way.

As we seek out the truth about the alleged 'mysteries' of Easter Island, let us begin with one of the earliest expeditions in modern times, that of 1914–15 led by the British ethnologist Katherine Routledge. In the Preface to her book *The Mystery of Easter Island*, published in 1920, she wrote:

> The facts now before us make clear that the present inhabitants of the island are derived from a union of the two great stocks of the Pacific, the Melanesian and Polynesian races, and that the Melanesian element has played a large part in its development. All the evidence gathered, whether derived from stone remains, through the surviving natives, or in other ways, points to the conclusion that these people are connected by blood with the makers of the statues; this is, of course, the crucial point.
>
> Now that this stage is reached, the problem at once falls into its right category, and we enter on the second phase of scientific quest. Easter Island is no longer an isolated mystery, there is no need to indulge in surmises as to sunken continents, it becomes part of the whole question of the culture of the

Pacific and of the successive waves of migration which have passed through it.[5]

Concerning the statues themselves, Mrs Routledge found ample evidence of the means of their construction. The stone tools used to carve them were found in great abundance lying around the quarries of *Rano Raraku*, an extinct volcano. The material for the statues is a reddish-brown or grey volcanic tuff (which is relatively soft) and the tools were fashioned from a harder, compact basalt. Most of the stone picks are of a teardrop design but a few are adze-like with the working edge bevelled off (like a chisel) and the top abraded as if struck by a mallet (see illus 31). Although von Däniken found the volcanic rock to be 'steel hard', the prehistoric islanders did not. This is what von Däniken considers to be the most important issue: the 'mysterious' fact that the statues were ever carved out of the 'steel hard' volcanic rock in the first place.[6] Surely, he reasons, such an enormous job could not have been accomplished with these primitive stone tools found in the local quarry.

In 1955–6, the Norwegian explorer-anthropologist Thor Heyerdahl led an expedition of archaeologists to Easter Island for the purpose of finding the answers to this and other puzzles. And on this expedition, which lasted six months, not only was the carving process demonstrated by the islanders themselves, but the transporting and raising of one of the statues onto its *ahu* platform was demonstrated as well (see illus 32–37).

In carving a statue, the initial step was to soften the surface of the stone with an application of water. Each carver kept at his side a gourd of water for this purpose. He would splash it on as needed to help penetrate the hard outer layer of the volcanic ash. Once through this tough exterior, the carving went much faster. Also, a very skilful flaking motion was used, with the basalt tool, to cut a pair of grooves in the rock, leaving a keel in the middle which was later knocked out, The result was an extremely efficient process by which six men, in the Heyerdahl experiment, were able to carve the entire outline around a medium-size statue in just three days. Archaeologists on the expedition later calculated that the complete job, using the same number of men but

73

in double-shifts, would take about one year. Interestingly enough, Katherine Routledge arrived at a similar conclusion back in 1914. She said: 'The whole process was not necessarily very lengthy; a calculation of the number of men who could work at the stone at the same time, and the amount each could accomplish, gave the rather surprising result that a statue might be roughed out within the space of fifteen days.'[7]

Of course, it adds to the 'mystery' if you accept von Däniken's population estimate of 2,000 islanders (working for – how long?). But, the truth is – no archaeologist I know of agrees with that figure. The generally accepted population figure for Easter Island in prehistoric times is more like three or four thousand, and perhaps it was even as high as twenty thousand people. In answer to von Däniken's claim that the island could not have supported a population of 2,000, for lack of food, Heyerdahl estimates that the island could easily have fed twenty thousand people.[8]

When I asked University of Arizona ethnologist Edwin Ferdon (who was also a member of the Heyerdahl expedition) about this problem, he told me that, although the island may appear to be barren, it has very good rainfall and the natives grow taro and sweet potatoes there in large quantities.[9]

The prehistoric islanders also had domesticated chickens, fish, bananas, sugar cane, yams, and a species of edible rat (called *kio'e*). As the real facts are presented, it becomes obvious that von Däniken has either fabricated his account of prehistoric Easter Island, or else he must be an exceedingly poor researcher.

The transporting of the statues is likewise no mystery. In another experiment conducted on the Heyerdahl expedition, a twelve-ton statue was transported over a long distance by 180 men pulling ropes attached to the stone giant's head while the body rested on a wooden sled.

Another statue, this one weighing about twenty or thirty tons, was raised onto a masonry platform. This was done through the use of levers (three large wooden poles) and an ingenious under-building of stones. It took twelve men eighteen days to complete the job – the point, of course, being that outer-space technology was not required.

As usual, von Däniken's 'mysteries' are derived from a distortion of the facts. A careful reading of *Chariots of the Gods?* reveals a humorous inconsistency. On page 113 he speaks of the 'wooden tablets, [called *rongorongo* boards] covered with strange hieroglyphs' that were 'found on some of the statues', but then on page 114 states that 'no trees grow on the island'; therefore they must have been transported 'without rollers'. First he says the islanders *did* have wood, and then he tells us they didn't!

The Easter Islanders did indeed have wood (for *rongorongo* boards, other small carvings of figurines, levers, sleds, and rollers) as well as the local *hau* (*Triumfetta semitriloba*) bast, with which to make rope. The tough reeds can be used to make cordage of any size by retwisting several smaller ropes together. Furthermore, pollen studies have shown that a much denser tree cover existed on Easter Island in earlier times, in contrast with what is mostly grassland today.

Clearly, the prehistoric islanders had both the physical resources and ingenuity to accomplish what von Däniken still refuses to give them credit for.

SOURCE NOTES

1 Erich von Däniken, *In Search of Ancient Gods* (London: Corgi Books, 1976), pp114–15.
2 *Chariots of the Gods?* p113.
3 Ibid., pp114–15.
4 *Playboy*, August 1974, p51.
5 Katherine Routledge, *The Mystery of Easter Island* (London: Sifton, Praed & Co., 1920), pxii.
6 *Chariots*, p114.
7 *The Mystery of Easter Island*, p81.
8 From a transcript of the BBC television documentary *The Case of the Ancient Astronauts*, first aired in the United States as part of the NOVA series on 8 March 1978.
9 For the complete interview with Ed Ferdon, see my first book, *The Space-Gods Revealed* (London: New English Library, 1977), pp48–55.

Von Däniken creates similar 'mysteries' for ancient Egypt as he does for Easter Island. Again, he tells us that archaeologists do not know from where the local people came; that their population was too small to provide the necessary manpower to create great monuments in stone; that there was not enough food to support a very large population; that no wood was available for 'rollers' with which to move large stones; that 'primitive' methods could not have been used to construct such miracles as the pyramids.

First, concerning the status of Egyptian history: not only do we have an abundance of artifacts and pictorial remains (which all happen to contradict the ancient astronaut theory) but since the discovery of the Rosetta Stone in 1799, and subsequent deciphering by Champollion, Egyptian hieroglyphics can be translated to such a high degree of accuracy that we are left with little to guess at. In fact, there exists such a wealth of knowledge on ancient Egypt, that no one scholar can master it all in one lifetime.

Origins of the Egyptian people can be traced back more than 5,000 years, in an unbroken line, from the Fayum period (representing settled village life and the vestiges of agriculture) up through the rulerships associated with the construction of the pyramids. Evidence of Sumerian, Babylonian, Hebrew, and Mesopotamian influence, among others, is likewise clearly established.

Speaking of the inhabitants of Egypt, during the time the Great Pyramid of Cheops was constructed, von Däniken asks:

'Could they all . . . have lived on the scanty yields of agriculture in the Nile delta?'[1]

'Several hundred thousand workers pushed and pulled blocks weighing 12 tons up a ramp with (non-existent) grain,'[2] he says. And, according to von Däniken . . . 'the Egyptians would scarcely have felled and turned into rollers the few trees, mainly palms, that then (as now) grew in Egypt, because the dates from the palms were urgently needed for food . . .'[3] The truth is that barley and wheat grew in abundance in the rich mud silt left by the annual flooding of the Nile. Tomb paintings abound that show the early Egyptians harvesting and storing grain, herding cattle, caring for flocks of geese, hauling in large quantities of fish in fishing boats, and making wine (see illus 38–42). In fact, Egyptians had more food than they could use themselves and went to market with much of it to trade for other goods.

The whole point of the Sirius-based calendar, which seems so troublesome for von Däniken, was that the appearance of this star (the brightest in the night sky) signalled the beginning of the flood season that was so vital to Egypt's agricultural system. Von Däniken writes: 'Sirius was one of the few stars they [the ancient Egyptians] took an interest in. But this very interest in Sirius seems rather peculiar, because seen from Memphis [the ancient capital of Egypt], Sirius can be observed only in the early dawn just above the horizon when the Nile floods begin. To fill the measure of confusion to overflowing, there was an accurate calendar in Egypt 4,221 years before our era! This calendar was based on the rise of Sirius . . .'[4]

This may be mysterious to von Däniken, but not to an Egyptian farmer. Almost all of Egypt's food came from the fertile land bordering on the Nile. Each year the most important event for food growers and for the Egyptian economy was the flooding of the Nile. Human ingenuity, especially when applied towards making a living, has been demonstrated in the recorded histories of the past, and we can see it all around us today. It's hardly 'peculiar', then, that the ancient Egyptian astronomers took an interest in Sirius, whose appearance signalled the start of the Nile flood, so important for their economy, and developed a calendar based on it.

The overall false picture of ancient Egypt created by von Däniken, of course, helps to heighten the mystery of how the Great Pyramid was built. It is true, of course, that had no wood been available in Egypt with which to make rollers or sledges, we would be left with no explanation of how the huge stones, used to construct the Great Pyramid, could have been transported and moved into place. But, again, the truth is that trade expeditions were common in which cedar wood was imported from Lebanon. The Egyptians also had sycamore, cypress, and other native and foreign woods (see illus 43–45). Cedar wood beams are found inside several of the pyramids and wood was used in making many of the everyday items used by Egyptian peasants, such as hoes and sickles, which are pictured on tomb walls and temples.

Most significant of all are the discoveries of several large wooden boats found in rock-cut boat pits alongside some of the larger pyramids. In May 1954, it was announced that a 140-foot vessel, made of cedar wood from Lebanon, was discovered in a boat pit on the south side of the Great Pyramid. The boat had been carefully taken apart (in 1,200 pieces) and stored together with several thousand feet of rope. These priceless artifacts are in a state of almost perfect preservation after having been sealed up in the airtight chamber for over 4,500 years.[5]

The next question to be answered is how '2,600,000 gigantic 12-ton blocks were cut out of the quarries, dressed and transported . . .'[6] in order to build the Great Pyramid of Cheops. First, let's use the true figures: the average weight of each block is closer to $2\frac{1}{2}$ tons (although a few weigh up to 15 tons), not 12 tons as von Däniken states. Also, the total number of blocks used in the Great Pyramid is estimated at 2,300,000 and its true dimensions are 445 feet (or 137 metres) in height, 738 feet (or 227 metres) on each side and it covers a ground area of 13 acres. The slope angle of the sides is approximately 52°.[7] Leading up to the Great Pyramid from the bank of the Nile is an enormous causeway half a mile in length, 60 feet wide and, at its highest point, 48 feet high. The causeway, which according to Herodotus was used for the conveyance of the stones, would surely not have been required by ancient astronauts.

The stone-cutting was accomplished not with lasers, but with copper chisels and saws (the cutting edges of which were hardened by adding quartz sand during the smelting process). Also used were chipping tools made of flint, and hammers, the heads of which were made from a very hard rock called diorite.

Local quarries still bear the rough cut-marks left by these tools along with evidence of the use of fire-cracking and water-based methods of simplifying the cutting of limestone, which is a relatively soft rock. Wooden wedges, soaked in water, would be hammered into grooves which would later expand and split off the rock. One such demonstration was filmed and shown on television recently (in 1978) in a documentary, entitled *The Case of the Ancient Astronauts*, produced by the BBC (and featured on the NOVA series in the United States, first aired on 8 March 1978).

Most of the stone used was limestone, available in huge quantities in the immediate vicinity. A better grade, used for some of the interior work, came from quarries near Memphis. The outer casing, a fine, white limestone, was obtained from Tura (about 15 miles distant on the eastern bank of the Nile) and granite used for the sarcophagus was quarried at Aswan and floated down the Nile on barges for a distance of 600 miles (see illus 46–48).

The usual method of transporting large stones over land was to load them on sledges which were pulled by dozens of men with ropes. Other workers poured liquid (water, some kind of natural oil or possibly even milk) under the sledges to make the ground slippery, to cut down on friction. According to scenes painted on tomb walls, levers were also used to help reduce the weight of the stones as the sledges were pulled along (see illus 49).

To get the stones in place, long ramps of earth and rubble were constructed against the sides of the pyramids. About this, there is little doubt, since some of the ramps have been found still in place. The ramps were usually removed upon completion of the structure, but at the unfinished Step Pyramid at Saqqara, for example, the ramps are still there.

Von Däniken says that: 'Today, in the twentieth century, no architect could build a copy of the Pyramid of Cheops, even if the technical resources of every continent were at his disposal.'[8]

Well, we certainly could, but it would be a terribly expensive job. We could replace stone chisels with jackhammers, and teams of struggling workmen hauling large stones with hydraulic trucks; bulldozers could do a quick job of levelling the base. But, as one Japanese construction firm has estimated, it would cost about $563 million, using modern technology to cut the time required for the job down to five years. Officials of Ohbayashi-Gumi said that if 200,000 workmen were hired over a period of thirty years at today's labour rates, the cost would be around $18 billion.[9]

Of course it helps the case for the Space-Gods if magnificent achievements seem to appear 'overnight', which is the impression von Däniken tries to create over and over again. But not only can we trace the origins of the Egyptian people; but also the development of their pyramid-building techniques.

The fact is that the pyramids did not just 'shoot out of the ground', so to speak. Like most other aspects of civilisation, pyramid-building was a gradual process, one idea leading to another. The earliest royal tombs are called 'mastabas', because they resembled the shape of brick benches of that name found outside many houses in Egyptian villages. They were simply mud-brick constructions formed in the shape of a large rectangle. Each mastaba had under it a burial chamber plus other chambers and storerooms. Such structures were used for royal burials from the First Dynasty (c 3100 BC) until the start of the Third Dynasty (c 2780 BC). And as the mastabas became more elaborate with additional chambers and other embellishments, techniques in stone-working also improved. So much so, that the Step Pyramid of Zoser (c 2700 BC) became the first royal monument to be built entirely of stone.

King Zoser's architect was Imhotep*, who became legendary

---

*For a bit of humour, see *In Search of Ancient Mysteries*, Corgi Books, 1974, by Alan and Sally Landsburg, who imply that Imhotep was an extraterrestrial. Actially, he was born in the village of Gebelein, south of Luxor, and was the son of Ka-nefer, then Director of Works of Upper and Lower Egypt. Imhotep was indeed popular during his lifetime, and if he were around today we would surely see him as a frequent guest on the Johnny Carson *Tonight Show*.

as a magician and physician, as well as the inventor of stone-masonry in Egypt. Zoser's Step Pyramid at Saqqara was actually six mastabas superimposed, one on the other, and represented the first major step towards a true pyramidal design. After this had been done, it was a fairly simple matter, at least on a relatively small scale, to fill in between the steps to form a true pyramid. And it did not take much to realise that what could be done with a small model could probably be accomplished on a much larger scale.

Then came the first true pyramid – the ruined Pyramid of Meidum. The experiment ended in disaster with part of the structure collapsing from its own weight. Improvements were again made, resulting in a new monument for King Sneferu (*c* 2680 BC) – the bent Pyramid of Dahshur. Surely, such trial and error methods are not befitting the advanced technology of Space-Gods! Sneferu's son and successor was Khufu (or Cheops), for whom the Great Pyramid at Giza was built. The Great Pyramid, then, was the culmination of centuries of development and experiment (see illus 50–56). Shortly thereafter, ancient Egypt entered a decadent stage, and eventually the carefully refined techniques of the pyramid-builders became a lost art.

One honest question often raised is – why, if the pyramids were meant only as royal tombs, are mummies not found in all of them? I would say, first of all, that the pyramids were intended by the kings who had them built as *monuments*, first and foremost, and second as tombs. Of course, there might also have been religious reasons about which we know nothing, but another explanation for the lack of original burials is that some mummies were moved out of the pyramids to foil grave robbers. Egyptologist Ahmed Fakhry (in his book *The Pyramids*, 1961) tells of a 'time of weakness and unrest called the First Intermediate period' which 'may have led to a story related by Diodorus, who wrote that the Egyptians so hated the builders of the pyramids that they threatened to enter these great tombs and destroy the mummies of the kings'.[10]

It would be an oversimplification to ascribe the building of these gigantic monuments merely to the soaring egos of the kings, as there were very good religious reasons (which made sense to the ancient Egyptians) as well. A fundamental consideration was the assumed connection between the well-being of the deceased ruler in the after-life, among the other immortal souls and gods of all kinds, and the general welfare of all his surviving subjects.

One of the assurances of immortality for the king (or so the Egyptians thought) was the practice of mummification (see illus 57–59). Von Däniken views mummification as a way to preserve bodies so that the gods can come back from outer space and awaken the sleeping dead. He compares this technique to Robert C. W. Ettinger's concept (described in his book *The Prospect of Immortality*) of preserving bodies in deep freeze and defrosting them when the diseases from which they died are curable. Such a comparison might have made sense were it not for some facts (which von Däniken neglected to mention) about the ancient embalming process.

The first thing Egyptian priests did to prepare a corpse for mummification was pull its brain out of its nose with a long pair of copper tweezers – bit by bit. Then its viscera (lungs, stomach, liver, spleen, etc) were extracted and placed in four canopic jars. Only the heart remained as it was thought to be the seat of the soul. Body cavities were washed with palm wine and given a coat of liquid resins to help keep away parasites such as fungi and insects. (The mummy of Ramses II was discovered to have both, when examined in 1974, and modern measures had to be taken to eliminate them.)[11] Then the body was soaked in a salt solution before receiving the final coats of hot liquid resin and several hundred feet of linen wrappings. All in all, the treatment was surely not one that any sensible doctor (or prudent extraterrestrial) would use to preserve himself for a corporeal return to life.

SOURCE NOTES
1 *Chariots of the Gods?* p97.
2 Ibid., p101.
3 Ibid., p97.

4 Ibid., pp85–6.
5 *National Geographic*, Vol 151, No 3, March 1977, p296.
6 *Chariots*, p100.
7 Ahmed Fakhry, *The Pyramids* (Chicago: University of Chicago Press, 1961), p115.
8 *Chariots*, p100.
9 *Arizona Daily Star*, 4 June 1978.
10 *The Pyramids*. p99.
11 *Newsweek*, 11 October 1976, p54.

The oldest examples of pictorial art performed by human beings are the rock paintings found throughout the world, which date from 60,000 to 10,000 BC. The earliest efforts are simple outlines and line drawings from the Aurignacian period (60,000 to 40,000 BC) which gradually evolve through clearly marked stages, during the Solutrean (40,000 to 30,000 BC), climaxing in the very elaborate polychrome paintings of the Magdalenian (30,000 to 10,000 BC) culture-phase.

The subject matter for most rock pictures was taken from daily life, depicting hunting scenes in the vast majority of caves; other drawings are clearly related to magical and religious rites. Oftentimes, the two categories are combined just as the everyday *lives* of primitive people *are* bound-up inseparably with magic and religion. We find many scenes that depict the magicians themsleves, wearing animal masks and headgear appropriate for the cult-dances which they performed. Such descriptions, however, do not satisfy von Däniken, who insists on identifying any kind of shamanistic headgear as space helmets and/or radio antennae.*

*I received the following comment from Mr Otto F. Reiss, editor and publisher of the *Art and Archaeology Newsletter*, 243 East 39th Street, New York NY 10016: 'Only the earliest forms of our walkie talkie headsets (in the 1940s and 1950s) had horn-like antennas. By the time the Apollo astronauts did their stuff, such antennas had become superfluous. It is an amusing touch that Däniken's oh-so-superior astro-gods are stuck with the outdated Earth technology of 30 years ago.'

Contrary to what von Däniken would have us believe, ritual magic is not just something dreamed up by anthropologists to help 'explain away' unsolved mysteries of the past. All sorts of magical rites and primitive religions can still be observed today in what are called contemporary 'stone-age' cultures. These modern-day 'primitives' worship some of the same 'gods' and perform similar ceremonies as their ancestors did, thousands of years ago.

The headdresses and masks worn by priests and magicians are not without purpose. To begin with, the personage wearing such garb appeared far more menacing and powerful than he would have if he were dressed just like an ordinary man. It is also well-known that the individual elements of design that comprise a mask or headdress each have their own special significance, meaningful only to the practitioners of that particular religion or cult. One thing is certain: to understand fully any ancient drawing (as with an artifact), it must not be taken in isolation, but rather considered *in context* with every circumstance known to be associated with it.

Perhaps the most famous of all rock paintings interpreted by von Däniken as that of an astronaut is the so-called Tassili 'Martian'. Discovered by the French archaeologist Henri Lhote in the Tassili N'Ajjer mountains of the Central Sahara, in 1956, the 'Great Martian God of Jabbaren' was found along with several thousand other examples of early Negroid art. Von Däniken says: 'Without overstretching my imagination, I get the impression that the great god Mars is depicted in a space- or diving-suit. On his heavy powerful shoulders rests a helmet which is connected to his torso by a kind of joint. There are a number of slits on the helmet where mouth and nose would normally be.'[1] A more fitting description of the painting might be as follows: the figure shown gives the immediate impression of a Cyclops from ancient Greek mythology. It appears to have a large 'eye' in the centre of its forehead and another smaller one off-centre on the side of its face (see illus 60). It is wearing a loose-fitting garment that looks something like a football jersey with shoulder pads underneath. Neck bands are depicted as on many other Tassili frescoes. What von Däniken calls a 'helmet' looks more like a sultan's turban, to me. Could it be possible that the clothing worn by the personage of that particular painting might in fact be a ritual mask and costume?

Von Däniken does not bother to let the readers in on what was found *in association with* the painting of the 'Martian God' – so allow me. As is typical in most instances of rock art, hunting and fighting scenes are most prominent, accompanied by renderings of the more mundane aspects of everyday life. In some cases the 'space-helmeted' figures are women (denoted by their conical pendulous breasts) carrying baskets on their heads (interpreted by von Däniken as antennae) (see illus 61). Other 'astronauts', shooting bows and arrows, are wearing 'helmets' that bear an uncanny resemblance to skull caps with feathers sticking out of them (see illus 62).

Most of the Tassili frescoes referred to by von Däniken are from an artistic tradition appropriately called the 'Period of the Round Heads', which dates back to between 8,000 and 6,000 BC. In conjunction with the artwork of this period are found Old Stone Age tools, weapons and other artifacts, which testify to the level of technology and general culture traits of the local inhabitants. Not a single ray-gun or any other space-age device has, to date, been unearthed in the Sahara, nor anywhere else on Earth for that matter.

Furthermore, I think it should be up to von Däniken to explain why space helmets need be worn by persons who are otherwise naked. The vast majority of his 'space-suited' figures collected from all over the world are similarly 'depressurised' (oftentimes having their sexual organs exposed). These include the Tassili frescoes, some of the Dogu statuettes from Japan, rock paintings at Nourlangie Rock, Australia, and many others. Less far-fetched than the theories of von Däniken, and backed by more abundant evidence as well, is the idea that this 'X-rated' kind of art was derived in each instance from a local fertility cult.

SOURCE NOTE
1 *Chariots of the Gods?* p48.

Due to the diverse 'evidence' that von Däniken cites in support of the ancient astronaut theory, a chapter of *miscellaneous* items is unavoidable in a book such as this – so here it is. Obviously, it would be virtually impossible to include *everything* he talks about, especially in view of the fact that he seldom gives references to aid the researcher who may wish to investigate further. To refute someone like von Däniken on every point would take far more space than his original statements, which would be impractical.

HELWAN CLOTH

In *Chariots of the Gods?* we are told that, 'In Helwan there is a piece of cloth, a fabric so fine that it could only be woven today in a special factory with great technical know-how and experience.'[1] The truth is that we not only have the gauze and linen that the ancient Egyptians wove, but also the wooden looms that they used to weave it with (see illus 64). Nor was the art of weaving fine cloth a sudden development, as we might be led to believe. The Anatolians, 2,000 years earlier, had begun developing the methods that were to evolve over those many years.

*

*For explanations of other miscellaneous 'mysteries' not included here, such as the Tiahuanaco Calendar, Baghdad Batteries, Iron Pillar of Meharauli, Rock Drawings of the Quechan Indians, and Moons of Mars, please see my first book, *The Space-Gods Revealed*, New English Library, London, 1977.

COTTON IN PERU

Similarly, von Däniken states that, 'It is an absolute mystery to us why the Incas cultivated cotton in Peru in 3000 BC although they did not know or possess the loom!'[2] For one thing, the Incas did not arrive on the scene until the fifteenth century AD, just before the Spanish conquest. But the Peruvians of 3000 BC, who were *not* Incas, cultivated cotton, which they used by twining and plaiting it. The later Incas did have looms, which remain as artifacts today.

PIRI RE'IS MAP

Another ancient accomplishment which von Däniken finds amazing is an early map of the world (of which we only have a portion) claimed to be

> ... absolutely accurate – and not only as regards the Mediterranean and the Dead Sea. The coasts of North and South America and even the contours of the Antarctic were also precisely delineated on Piri Reis's maps. The maps not only reproduced the outlines of the continents, but also showed the topography of the interiors! Mountain ranges, mountain peaks, islands, rivers, and plateaus were drawn in with extreme accuracy . . . Comparison with modern photographs of our globe taken from satellites showed that the originals of Piri Reis's maps must have been aerial photographs taken from a very great height.[3]

Nothing could better illustrate von Däniken's method of presenting false information to the reader as his account of the Piri Re'is map. The singular map shown in *Chariots of the Gods?* was found in 1929 in the old palace of Topkapi as it was being converted into a museum. It is dated 1513, and all of the marginal notes that appear on the map have been translated.* The complete story of

*The interested reader can find them reprinted on pp220–4 of Charles H. Hapgood's book *Maps of the Ancient Sea Kings*, Chilton Books, Philadelphia and New York, 1966.

its origin is told thereon, and virtually nothing von Däniken says about the map is true.

Piri Re'is, a Turkish admiral and noted cartographer of his day, drew the map from about twenty other charts which he reduced to one scale. And in so doing, certain errors appeared, which testify clearly to his limited knowledge of the geography of the world. These errors include: the omission of about 900 miles of South American coastline, a duplication of the Amazon River, the omission of the Drake Passage between Cape Horn and the Antarctic Peninsula (representing nine degrees on the map), and a non-existent landmass (presumed by some present-day occultists to be Atlantis) that is drawn about 4,000 miles north of where Antarctica should be. Neither the Mediterranean nor the Dead Sea appear on the map at all (see illus 65–67). This says nothing of the fact that none of the mountain ranges, islands, rivers, nor coastlines are drawn true to form (especially when it comes to matching up the southernmost portion of the map with Antarctica). In other words, the map fits in perfectly well with other sixteenth century cartography and in no way can it be reasonably interpreted as the product of space-beings engaged in prehistoric aerial reconnaissance. Once again, we must fight off the natural urge to indulge in wishful thinking and be on guard against believing the distortions of Erich von Däniken.

THE ANTIKYTHERA DEVICE

In 1900, just off the little island of Antikythera (between Crete and Kythera at the western entrance to the Aegean Sea), Greek sponge divers discovered the wreck of an ancient ship that had apparently sunk some time around 65 BC. The ship's cargo consisted mainly of art objects, sculpted from marble and bronze, which had probably been bound for Rome from either Rhodes or Cos. Among this hoard of art treasures was a remarkable bronze instrument, corroded and encrusted with calcareous deposits, but nonetheless recognisable as a clockwork mechanism containing some thirty gears of varying sizes and gear ratios all set in one parallel plane. There were also fragments of at least three dials, each with a number of scales and rotating slip rings. Although no pointers were found, some were probably used in conjunction with the dials. Most remarkable of all was a differential turntable, an innovation not previously encountered prior to the sixteenth century.

The whole mechanism, which was probably manufactured around 80 BC, seems to have been a calendrical calculator, perhaps operated by a folding crank. The American historian of science Derek de Solla Price of Yale University has conducted detailed studies on the device since the early 1950s, and has come to the conclusion that the ancient Greek 'computer', as he calls it, served as a miniature planetarium giving the past, present, and future positions of the sun and moon, including the cycle of the moon's phases (called the synodic month).

Von Däniken mentions the Antikythera device (in *Chariots of the Gods?*) as if it were an extraterrestrial artifact.[4] Of course it was a proud accomplishment of the ancient Greeks, but falls far short of what might reasonably be expected from a race of interplanetary space voyagers.

LITTLE GOLD AIRPLANES

In *The Gold of the Gods*, von Däniken mentions (and proudly displays illustrations of) another old favourite of ancient astronaut believers – the so-called little gold 'airplanes' from the collection of the Colombian National Museum in South America.[5] It is true that the thousand-year-old golden trinkets do *look like* miniature delta-wing jets, but the suggestive, superficial resemblance is disappointingly – just that. Although several variations of these artifacts exist, and in spite of their highly stylised appearance, they all have clearly recognisable features of either the Pacific 'flying fish', in some cases, or the 'devil fish' (*Manta birostris* of the ray family), in others (see illus 68, 69). Each has the characteristic fish-head with two eyes, fins, and protruding tail. It is, of course, fun to play 'it looks like', but the 'gullibility factor' is one to consider in this case.

THE CABRERA STONES

Almost as tantalising as the supposed 'ancient jets' are the engraved stones found in the privately owned museum called the 'House of Culture' in Ica, Peru, belonging to Dr Janvier Cabrera Darquea. Himself a surgeon, it is little wonder that Dr Cabrera found these artifacts interesting, since they show, among other medical operations, heart and brain transplants being performed back in the days of the dinosaurs! Other scenes depict men looking through telescopes at the heavens, examining rocks or fossils with a magnifying glass, men attacking a dinosaur, etc. Naturally, Carbrera claims that the stones are thousands (indeed, why not millions?) of years old, *proving* that ancient astronauts came to Earth and established a technologically advanced era in days gone by.

Von Däniken discovered the Cabrera stone in Robert Charroux's book *The Mysteries of the Andes* (see illus 70) and, *after learning that the stones were probably forgeries*, set off for Peru. (This, von Däniken admits, in his own book *According to the Evidence*.)[6] When von Däniken arrived at the museum, Dr Cabrera greeted him warmly and began showing the god-seeker his proud collection. Sure enough, more than 11,000 stones were stacked on shelf after shelf, from the floor to the ceiling, reminding von Däniken of an 'egg-shop'. Naturally, the blind and stodgy archaeological community had no interest in the mind-boggling engravings, so Cabrera was delighted that at least von Däniken could recognise solid scientific evidence when he saw it.

When a film crew of the BBC arrived, to shoot some footage for their documentary *The Case of the Ancient Astronauts*, they did not receive such a warm welcome. They were refused permission to photograph the collection, and Cabrera even refused to discuss his extraordinary scientific evidence. Surprisingly, however, he handed over one stone, claimed to be very old and genuine, to the BBC to keep as a souvenir of their visit. The stone was subsequently examined by the Institute of Geological Sciences in London and found to be a modern forgery, just as von Däniken had been informed, prior to his trip to Peru. The Institute reported (after microscopic examination): 'The sharp and relatively clean-cut edges of the grooves are notable, a feature which could not be preserved for long under normal weathering conditions.' Concerning the outer surface layer of the stone, which had oxydised and turned brown in colour, they said: 'The grooves are seen to cut into this surface layer, indicating a carving which *postdated* the development of the surface weathering.'[7]

The film crew was not surprised by this report, since they had already found the Ica artisan who had produced the stones, which he had sold to Cabrera and others. His name is Basilio, and he claims to have carved *all* of the stones in Cabrera's collection. As proof of this, he produced a local newspaper clipping, containing a photograph of Cabrera's museum on which a note was written and signed by Cabrera, thanking Basilio for providing the stones.

What are we going to make of this? Could there be some kind of elaborate conspiracy going on, world-wide, within the scientific establishment to keep hidden some of the astounding 'evidence' that von Däniken has uncovered? But for what purpose? What could they possibly be trying to hide? And how could they possibly pull it off? Any ambitious professor, or college student for that matter, could easily obtain one of the Cabrera stones, for instance, and have it tested (or test it personally) to *prove* once and for all that conventional archaeology is wrong. Such a person would be a hero and eventually very probably a millionaire, due to the associated publicity. Any scientist would jump at the chance to revolutionise his field, if he or she thought there was a reasonable chance to do so. The very absence of such a happening provides a *prima facie* case *against* von Däniken's theories, no matter how many more fraudulent books and movies are produced, which continue to con the rubes.

SOURCE NOTES
1 *Chariots of the Gods?* p43.
2 Ibid., p116.
3 Ibid., pp29–30.
4 Ibid., pp128–9.
5 *The Gold of the Gods*, pp36–8.
6 Erich von Däniken, *According to the Evidence*, trans. Michael Heron (London: Souvenir Press, 1977), p321.
7 From the BBC documentary, *The Case of the Ancient Astronauts*.

94

Shortly after sunrise (about 7.15 am), on the morning of 30 June 1908, a 'ball of fire' was seen, by some of the few inhabitants of the Central Siberian Plateau, coming over the southern horizon heading almost due north. The 'object' reportedly glowed with an intense bluish-white light – more dazzling than the sun – and possessed a streaming white tail.

Within a few seconds, it disappeared into the swampy wilderness of the Tunguska Taiga (forest), where it unleashed a titanic explosion, the equivalent of a multi-megaton nuclear bomb. After the initial flash of light, a 'pillar of fire' shot upwards into the sky, which could be seen from Kirensk, 250 miles away. Then, enormous black clouds rose twelve miles into the air, followed by 'black rain'. On the following day – and for three successive nights – ghostly glowing clouds were seen at extremely high altitudes, over Asia and Europe. The tremendous shock-wave of the blast circled the globe twice and was recorded on seismographs and barographs at Potsdam and London.

Originally, scientists thought an exceptionally large meteorite had impacted near the Podkamennaya (stony) Tunguska River producing the mammoth explosion. But when the first full-scale scientific expedition – led by mineralogist Leonid A. Kulik (1883–1942) – arrived at the blast-site in 1927*, they were puzzled

*Kulik led an earlier (and smaller) expedition into the area, in 1921, but had to turn back due to the illness and exhaustion of his companions. The later expeditions, of 1927 and 1938–9, were better equipped to deal with the extreme conditions encountered in the Siberian wilderness.

by the absence of a major crater, and could not find clearly identi-
fiable meteoric fragments as they had expected. What they did
find was a large swamp at the epicentre of the explosion, surrounded by bogs and marshes, and a devastated region of forest,
covering an area of hundreds of square miles. Within a twelve-
mile radius, trees had been levelled – some snapped off and others
uprooted. However, the most intense heat was confined to only
about a four-mile radius. In the next zone, extending out another
eight miles in all directions, were trees with less severe heat
damage – showing burns on the sides facing the centre of the
explosion – then another zone, averaging about ten miles farther
out, of trees that were toppled or stripped of limbs and branches,
due to the shock-wave, but without heat damage.

The 'mystery' of the Great Siberian Explosion now begins to
develop. Although Kulik always did believe that the cataclysm
was caused by a meteor, other grew doubtful. Without finding
pieces of the meteorite itself or, so the story goes, without even a
crater, Kulik's theory, apparently, had little evidence to support
it. What then could have happened on that fateful morning in
the summer of 1908?

It was not until 1945, after the nuclear bombing of Hiroshima
and Nagasaki, that the effects of atomic devices could be seen.
Some noticed, almost immediately, obvious parallels with the
Siberian explosion and brains began to tick. The blinding flash,
followed by a mushroom-shaped cloud (as some of the remaining
witnesses described the 'pillar of fire' associated with the Tunguska event), and a blast-pattern characteristic of a *mid-air* explosion (hence explaining the absence of a major crater). But
who could have built a nuclear device back in 1908? That's right
. . . *extraterrestrials*, of course!

In 1946, a Russian engineer and science-fiction writer by the
name of Alexandr Kazântsev took credit for this intriguing idea
by publishing the theory in the Soviet periodical *Vokrug Sveta*
(*Around the World*). His contention was that a crew of Martians
had attempted an emergency landing as their nuclear-powered
spaceship, intentionally headed for Earth, experienced technical
difficulties during the landing attempt. The energy pile exploded
and the spacecraft and its crew were instantly vaporised.

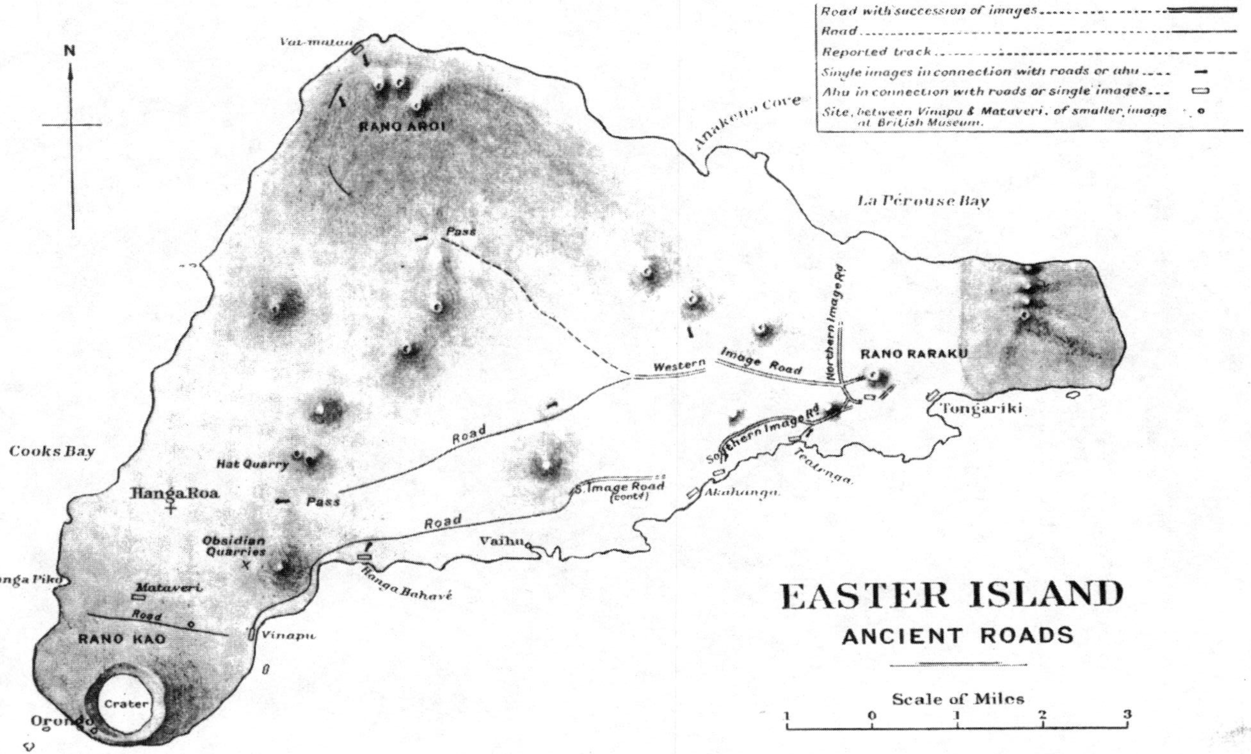
Road with succession of images
Road
Reported track
Single images in connection with roads or ahu
Ahu in connection with roads or single images
Site, between Vinapu & Mataveri, of smaller image at British Museum.
N
Vai-matau
RANO AROI
Anakena Cove
La Pérouse Bay
Pass
Western
Image Road
Northern Image Rd
RANO RARAKU
Tongariki
Southern Image Rd
Road
Cooks Bay
Hat Quarry
Teatenga
HangaRoa
Pass
S. Image Road (cont'd)
Akahanga
Road
Vaihu
Obsidian Quarries
Hanga Piko
Mataveri
Hanga Bahavé
Road
RANO KAO
Vinapu
Crater
Orongo
EASTER ISLAND
ANCIENT ROADS
Scale of Miles
1
0
1
2
3

28. Map of Easter Island. From *The Mystery of Easter Island,* by Katherine Routledge (London: Sifton, Praed & Co, 1920).

29

30

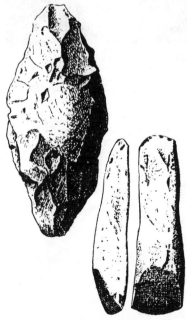

29. One of the earliest photographs ever taken by one of the brooding *moai*. From *The Mystery of Easter Island*, by Katherine Routledge.

30. Stone giants buried up to their necks by centuries of shifting sand and soil slippage caused by heavy rains. *Photo courtesy of Ed Ferdon and Thor Heyerdahl.*

31. The statue carvers' basalt tools found in the quarry at Rano Raraku. From *The Mystery of Easter Island.*

31

32. Heyerdahl's carving experiment — a close-up view. *Photo courtesy of Thor Heyerdahl.*

33. A twelve-ton statue being transported by about 180 natives. *Photo courtesy of Thor Heyerdahl.*

34. This 25- or 30-ton statue was raised on to its *ahu* platform in eighteen days by twelve men using only poles, stones, and ropes, all within the capabilities of Easter Island's prehistoric inhabitants. *Photo courtesy of Thor Heyerdahl.*

33

34

35. The lifting job completed, the statue rests on its *ahu* platform. The man beside it gives an idea of its size. *Photo courtesy of Thor Heyerdahl.*

36. This outline of a medium-size Easter Island Statue was accomplished by six men in just three days. It was estimated that if this small crew were to continue working for about one year, they could have finished the job. *Photo by Thor Heyerdahl.*

37 and 38. Paintings from an Egyptian tomb depicting an agricultural scene. From *History of Egypt,* Vol.3, by G. Maspero (London: The Grolier Society, 1906)

39. Hunting with the boomerang and fishing with the double-harpoon. From *History of Egypt,* Vol.2.

35

36

37

38

39

40. The cutting and carrying of the harvest. From *History of Egypt,* Vol.2.

41. Measuring the wheat and depositing it in the granaries. From *History of Egypt,* Vol.2.

42. Model of a granary. From *Life in Ancient Egypt* by Adolf Erman (London: Macmillan & Co., 1894)

43. Sycamore trees in Egypt (non-existent, according to von Däniken). From *Life in Ancient Egypt.*

44. Egyptian cargo-boat at the time of the Old Empire. From *Life in Ancient Egypt.*

45. An Egyptian trading vessel of the first half of the Eighteenth Dynasty. From *History of Egypt.*

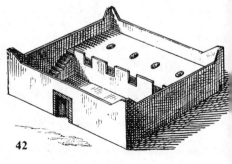

42

43

44

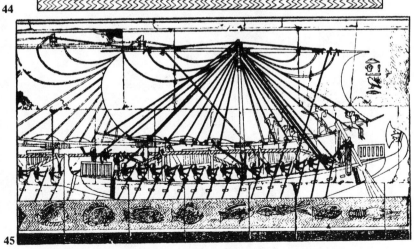

45

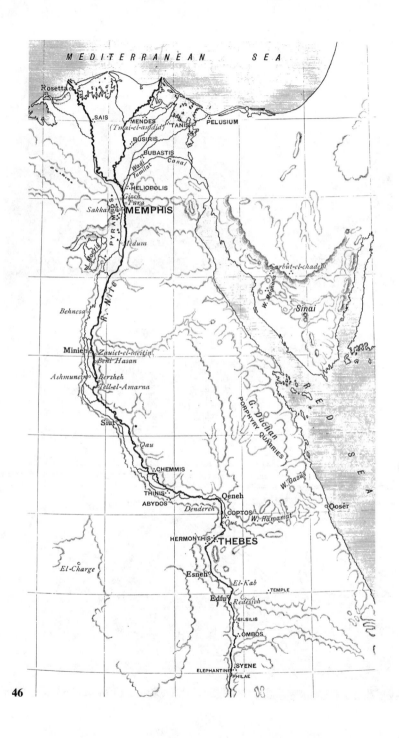

MEDITERRANEAN SEA

Rosetta

SAIS

MENDES
(Tmai-el-amdid)
BUSIRIS
TANIS
PELUSIUM

BUBASTIS

Wadi
Tumilat
Canal

HELIOPOLIS
Gizeh
Tura
Sakkarah
MEMPHIS

L. Moeris
PYRAMIDS
Medum

Serbut-el-chadem
W. Mughara

Sinai

Behnesa

R. Nile

Minieh
Zauiet-el-meitin
Beni Hasan
Ashmunein
Bersheh
Tell-el-Amarna

Siut

Qau

G. Dochan
PORPHYRY QUARRIES

CHEMMIS

THINIS
ABYDOS
Denderah
Qeneh
COPTOS
Qus
W. Hamamat

RED SEA

W. Gasus

Qoser

HERMONTHIS
THEBES

El-Charge

Esneh
El-Kab

Edfu
Redesieh
TEMPLE

SILSILIS

OMBOS

ELEPHANTINE
SYENE
PHILAE

46

47

46. Map of the Nile. From *Life in Ancient Egypt*.

47. The Pyramids of Gizeh, seen from the south. From *Life in Ancient Egypt*.

48. Stone-cutters finishing the dressing of limestone blocks. From *History of Egypt*, Vol.2.

48

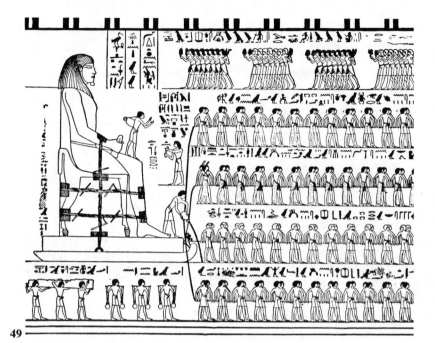

49

49. The colossal statue of Prince Thothotpu (weighing approximately 60 tons) being dragged by 172 men. From *History of Egypt,* Vol.3..

50. The mastaba of Khomtini in the necropolis of Gizeh. From *History of Egypt,* Vol.2.

51. Step-pyramid of Saggara. From *The Book of The Prophet Ezekiel,* by C.H. Toy (New York: Dodd, Mead & Co, 1899}.

52. The Ruined Pyramid of Meidum. From *History of Egypt,* Vol.1.

50

51

52

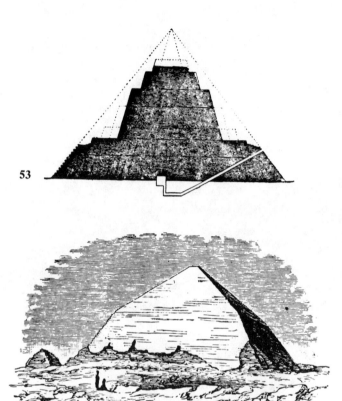

53. Pyramid of Meidum — a reconstructed view. From *History of Egypt,* Vol.2.

54. The Bent Pyramid of Dahshur. From *History of Egypt* Vol.1.

55. The Great Sphinx of Gizeh. From *A History of Egypt* by J. H. Breasted, London, 1921.

56. The Great Pyramids of Gizeh. From *A History of Egypt* (Breasted).

55

56

57. The art of
mummification. From
History of Egypt, Vol.4.

58 and 59. Coffin and face
of Ramses II. From *History
of Egypt,* Vol.2.

58

59

The Tunguska 'spaceship' theory is, sure enough, adopted by von Däniken in *Chariots of the Gods?*, while adding a claim that '. . . radioactivity around the centre of the explosion in the Taiga is twice as high – even today – as elsewhere.'[1] 'Tunguska-spaceship' proponents cite, as further evidence of this, the fact that pine trees in the Taiga began to grow faster *after* the great explosion than before.

Now let us take an *honest* look at what scientists have actually found in their investigations of the Tunguska event, and the reasoning used to arrive at a probable theory based on facts as opposed to science fiction. We will see how, once again – as in virtually all cases of pseudoscience and especially concerning 'theories' of ancient astronauts – important key information has been generally 'hidden' or withheld from all popular accounts (as opposed to scientific books and journals), in order to heighten the 'mystery'.

In the case of the Tunguska event, there was a special situation which contributed to its mystery status to begin with. And that is the fact that *nineteen years* had passed before the arrival of the Kulik expedition – so that much of the potential evidence of what really did happen there was simply gone. This point is especially relevant in this case because of the specific peculiarities of this particular spot. The site of the explosion (located near latitude 61° North and longitude 102° East) is in a region of forest and swamp, which is very near the Tundra zone. Ecologically speaking, this region is one of transition between Taiga (forest) and Tundra. Due to lack of natural water drainage, such regions become very swampy during the summer months with numerous temporary bogs and marshes, which convert from water to mud to solid frozen ground with each passing year. The whole region surrounding the area of devastation, for a radius of about fifteen miles, is extremely marshy and has many lakes. With the many downpours, snow storms, and high winds, taking place yearly in this region, it is highly likely that much decisive evidence was lost over a period of nineteen years – especially heavy iron fragments which are probably resting today far below the surface.

It is true that the limited drilling performed by several expeditions has not produced large chunks, but, by the same token, nor have any pieces of a space vehicle been found either. Many small nickel-iron globules (some five millimetres in diameter) were found however, in high concentration at the blast centre, which is characteristic of meteorites. (It is not commonly believed, even by the likes of Kazântsev and von Däniken, that supposed aliens build their spaceships out of nickel and iron! Or, if they did . . . it is easy to see why they would have trouble landing!) Moreover, a *nuclear-powered* spaceship (assuming the aliens had not discovered a more exotic energy source other than what we already know about) would likely be quite massive (perhaps even of the type that is assembled and operated only in deep space) and impractical for landing and take-off manoeuvres. Although nuclear engines may seem very far advanced to us Earth-folk in the twentieth century, they are not quite as versatile as many of us might think. The Tunguska 'spaceship' theory is actually not so exotic as it is simply far-fetched. The idea really *lacks* imagination just as much as it lacks evidence.

What is most appalling of all, in the many popular (and hence, money-making) versions of the Tunguska 'spaceship' theory, is the suppression of the most key fact of all, namely, the *craters* found at the site by Kulik back in 1927. Virtually every popular account of the Siberian explosion uses the absence of a major crater to help establish the 'mystery', *without mentioning* the fact that Kulik found (even nineteen years after the event) a group of ten craters, with diameters of about 30–160 feet and a mean depth of 13 feet, at the epicentre of the blast. There is even a photograph of one of these craters, which appeared in Fletcher G. Watson's book *Between the Planets* (see illus 71). Watson reports in his book that 'Under one crater . . . [Kulik] . . . found rock-flour and fused quartz containing minute grains of nickel-iron.'*

The item about abnormally high radioactivity in the area is

*New York: Blakiston, 1941, p168. The craters are also mentioned in an article entitled 'Meteorite Craters' in *Nature*, Vol 129, No 3265, 28 May 1932, pp781–3, and in C. Maxwell Cade and Delphine Davis's book *The Taming of the Thunderbolts*, Abelard-Schuman, London, 1969, p112.

also a matter of false or misleading information. According to the Russian geochemist Kirill P. Florensky, leader of the Tunguska expeditions of 1958, 1961, and 1962, there is nothing abnormal at all about the level of radiation found in the region and what radioactivity is found is likely '. . . fallout from modern atomic bombs . . .' and the rapid-growth of the trees is '. . . only the normal acceleration of second growth after fires had taken place. The meteorite had played only an indirect part in this acceleration.'[2]

Florensky thinks, as do I, that the evidence we do have points clearly to the conclusion that the Tunguska *meteorite* (a term which can be taken to mean any natural cosmic body falling to Earth) was more precisely the head of a small comet. And when all of the evidence, taken together, is considered objectively, there remains little doubt that Florensky is right. A few preliminary facts about comets will be helpful to our discussion in order to better understand the correlations with Tunguska.

Few cosmic bodies are as deceiving to the eye as are comets. While it may look like a fiery mass of molten matter, perhaps looking even as massive as a star, a comet is in reality a kind of celestial 'snowball' or as astronomer Percival Lowell (1855–1916) once put it: 'a bag-full of nothing'. Comets are actually great clouds of cosmic dust and meteoric (nickel and iron) chunks cemented together by frozen gases such as methane, carbon monoxide, and ordinary water-ice. In other words, highly volatile gases that are kept stable only because they have been deep-frozen for millions of years in the coldness of space. When a comet nears the sun, some of its dust and gas (in the form of minute frozen crystals) form its long tail, always forced away from the sun by the light pressure exerted by the 'solar wind'. It is likely that the 'noctilucent clouds' observed after the Tunguska blast were the remnants of the comet's tail. And if the comet was small enough and its orbital path near the line of sight to the sun, this would explain why it was not seen prior to entering the Earth's atmosphere.

When the comet did enter our atmosphere it is easy to understand how such an immense explosion could occur without the body itself striking the ground. The sudden deceleration in the air would, for one thing, cause the carbon monoxide and methane gas to sublimate, being instantly converted from the frozen to the gaseous state. This alone would result in a tremendous explosive force. Added to this, there would be immense heat generated by such a body falling at two miles per second; 'part of the released energy heats up the body, another part produces a shock wave'.[3] When such a loosely compacted body vaporises it leaves little remaining of its former presence. What has been found at Tunguska is just about what we would expect had a small comet arrived there on that frightful day.

SOURCE NOTES
1 *Chariots of the Gods?* p151.
2 Kirill P. Florensky, 'Did a Comet Collide with the Earth in 1908?' *Sky and Telescope*, Vol 26, No 5, November 1963, pp268–9.
3 Ibid., p269.

History records that 'strange' aerial objects have been haunted us Earthlings for thousands of years. Unknown lights and shapes seen in the sky – even tales of strange beings making contact with humans – these mysteries are a part of man's oldest art and literature. And, although we should view the early reports with caution, we cannot help but notice a certain appeal, that beckons our imagination and makes us want to believe that they might contain a kernel of truth.

'Fiery globes' fluttering about the night sky, 'circular shields' during the day – that is how the ancient Greeks and Romans described what they saw. The Egyptians of 3,500 years ago left accounts of 'circles of fire' and 'flaming chariots' that sailed across the heavens. The American Indians had their legends of 'flying canoes' and 'great silvery airships' in the days of the covered wagons. Such accounts have been handed down through the ages by nearly all peoples of the world: from ancient Egypt, India, Tibet, Japan, China, Scandinavia, Ireland, England, France, Italy, Polynesia and the Americas.

The following examples are quoted by Harold T. Wilkins, in his book *Flying Saucers on the Attack*, from supposedly ancient sources:

BC 216: Things like ships were seen in the sky, over Italy . . . At Apri (180 Roman miles east of Rome, in Apulia), a *round shield* was seen in the sky.

BC 214: The forms of ships were seen in the sky at Rome.

BC 213: At Hadria (Gulf of Venice), the strange spectacle of men with white clothing was seen in the sky. They seemed to stand around an altar, and were robed in white.

BC 170: At Lanupium (on the Appian Way, 16 miles from Rome), a remarkable spectacle of a fleet of ships was seen in the air.

BC 99: When C. Murius and L. Valerius were consuls, in Tarquinia, there fell in different places (about 52 Roman miles north-west of Rome, in Etruria), a thing like a flaming torch, and it came suddenly from the sky. Towards sunset, a round object like a globe, or round or circular shield (*orbis clypei*), took its path in the sky, from west to east.

BC 90: At Aenarie (an island in the Bay of Naples, now called Ischia), whilst Livius Troso (Drusus?) was promulgating the laws at the beginning of the Italian war . . . at sunrise, there came a terrific noise in the sky, and a globe of fire appeared burning in the north . . . Later, at Aenarie, the earth yawned open and a flame issued, which lit up all the country to the horizon. In the territory of Spoletum (65 Roman miles north of Rome, in Umbria), a globe of fire, of golden colour, fell to the earth, gyrating. It then seemed to increase in size, rose from the earth, and ascended into the sky, where it obscured the disc of the sun, with its brilliance. It resolved towards the eastern quadrant of the sky.

BC 75: A large natural stone (when the consuls were L. Martius and Sextus Julius), which rolled forward from a steep rock, suddenly stopped itself in the air, in the middle of its fall. It remained motionless.

AD 98: At Tarquinia, an old town in Campania, Italy, a burning torch was seen (*fax ardens*), all about the sky. It suddenly fell down. At sunset, a burning shield (*clypeus ardens*) passed over the sky at Rome. It came sparkling from the west and passed to the east.

AD 746 and 748: Dragons were seen in the sky . . . and ships in which men were seen in the air.[1]

102

In November 1969, there appeared an intriguing article entitled 'Paleolithic UFO Shapes', by the French ufologist Aimé Michel in the British *Flying Saucer Review* (Vol 15, No 6). Michel had found that our Magdalenian ancestors fashioned works of art that are striking indications that *they* too had seen UFOs. On the walls of the famous Les Eyzies, Laseaux, and Altamira caves in France and Spain, are found renderings of objects that somewhat resemble modern descriptions (and photographs) of disc-shaped UFOs (see figs and illus 72, 73, 74). The apparent similarity of these pictures to modern-day UFO reports captures our imagination instantly. One wonders how the Magdalenian artists, fifteen to thirty thousand years ago, could have envisioned the modern UFO phenomenon?

Whereas I am not adverse to the possibility of genuine UFO reports (even ancient ones), von Däniken has little to say about this. He concentrates instead on contact myths as indicated by this statement from *In Search of Ancient Gods*: 'I am firmly convinced that "gods" in mythology can only be a synonym for space travellers . . .'[2]

For example: the Aryans, a dominant race of ancient India, left us their sacred books called the *Vedas*. The *Vedas*, which are probably eight thousand years old, are collections of hymns, sacrificial rites, and liturgical texts. The gods, to whom the hymns were addressed, were celestial divinities, but almost human in some ways. Offerings were made of milk, honey-cakes, and a drink made of the fermented juice of *soma*, a psychedelic mush-room. One god was ruler of the lesser gods. And there were beings described as half-god and half-man. The *Vedas* contain what some people think might have been the first visitations of extra-terrestrials and their contact with ancient Earth-men.

Because these writings were originally composed in Sanskrit, which is often difficult to translate with a high degree of accuracy, it seems only fair to view various interpretations with an open mind. 'With thy light,' runs one of these old hymns, 'thou dost cover the earth which bareth mankind, thou dost flood the heavens and the vast air, and thou lookest upon all that doth exist. Seven tawny-haired mares draw thy chariot, O dazzling

Surya; their beautiful hair is crowned with rays of light, thou god who seest all things.'

Surya is interpreted by the translator as the sun, but in the *Vedas* this *Surya* is associated with celestial riders. The *Maruts* are usually interpreted in modern translations as 'storm' or 'wind' gods. But some scholars have noted that the word *marut* has much in common with the name Mars and other words that describe the colour red. Furthermore, the 'clouds', in which the *maruts* flew about, changed colour as they increased speed, as in many modern reports of UFOs. Another Indic 'myth', the *Mahabharata*, tells of flying vehicles called *vimanas* and, even more startling, what seems to have been an ancient atomic war.

It should be observed, however, that such material is vague and equivocal, and hence very difficult to translate and interpret correctly. And most of these accounts are just as convincingly interpreted as describing natural phenomena, which were not at all well understood by the ancients, giving rise to nature worship, which we might easily misinterpret today as evidence of 'gods' from outer space.

One 'Chaldean' legend, about a creature named Oannes, is even more intriguing to many people than the 'atomic wars' of ancient India. In fact, the American astronomer Carl Sagan once suggested, in his book *Intelligent Life in the Universe* (co-authored with the Soviet astronomer, I. S. Shklovskii), that the Oannes legend should receive '. . . much more critical studies than have been performed heretofore, with the possibility of direct contact with an extraterrestrial civilization as one of many possible alternative interpretations'.[3]

The legend is quoted by Sagan, from Cory's *Ancient Fragments* (1876), as follows:

The account of Alexander Polyhistor:
Berosus, in his first book concerning the history of Babylonia, informs us that he lived in the time of Alexander, the son of Philip. And he mentions that there were written accounts preserved at Babylon with the greatest care, comprehending a term of fifteen myriads of years. These writings contained a history of the heavens and the sea; of the birth of mankind;

also of those who had sovereign rule; and of the actions achieved by them.

And, in the first place, he describes Babylonia as a country which lay between the Tigris and Euphrates. He mentions that it abounded with wheat, barley, ocrus, sesamum; and in the lakes were found the roots called gongae, which were good to be eaten, and were, in respect to nutriment, like barley. There were also palm trees and apples, and most kinds of fruits; fish, too, and birds; both those which are merely of flight, and those which take to the element of water. The part of Babylon which bordered upon Arabia was barren, and without water; but that which lay on the other side had hills, and was fruitful. At Babylon there was (in these times) a great resort of people of various nations, who inhabited Chaldea, and lived without rule and order, like the beasts of the field.

In the first year there made its appearance, from a part of the Persian Gulf which bordered upon Babylonia, an animal endowed with reason, who was called Oannes. (According to the account of Appollodorus) the whole body of the animal was like that of a fish; and had under a fish's head another head, and also feet below, similar to those of a man, subjoined to the fish's tail. His voice, too, and language was articulate and human; and a representation of him is preserved even to this day [on an Assyrian cylinder seal].

This Being, in the day-time used to converse with men; but took no food at that season; and he gave them an insight into letters, and sciences, and every kind of art. He taught them to construct houses, to found temples, to compile laws, and explained to them the principles of geometrical knowledge. He made them distinguish the seeds of the earth, and showed them how to collect fruits. In short, he instructed them in everything which could tend to soften manners and humanise mankind. From that time, so universal were his instructions, nothing material has been added by way of improvement. When the sun set it was the custom of this Being to plunge again into the sea, and abide all night in the deep; for he was amphibious.

After this, there appeared other animals, like Oannes, of which Berosus promises to give an account when he comes to

105

the history of the kings. Moreover, Berosus wrote concerning the generation of mankind; of their different ways of life, and of their civil polity . . .

The account of Abydenus:

So much concerning the wisdom of the Chaldaeans.

It is said that the first king of the country was Alorus, who gave out a report that he was appointed by God to be the Shepherd of the people; he reigned ten sari. Now a sarus is esteemed to be three thousand six hundred years; a neros, six hundred: and a sossus, sixty.

After him Alaparus reigned three sari; to him succeeded Amillarus, from the city of Pantibiblon, who reigned thirteen sari; in his time a semi-daemon called Annedotus, very like to Oannes, came up a second time from the sea. After him Ammenon reigned twelve sari, who was from the city of Pantibiblon; then Megalarus, of the same place, eighteen sari; then Daos, the shepherd, governed for the space of ten sari – he was of Pantibiblon; in his time four double-shaped personages came out of the sea to land, whose names were Euedocus, Eneugamus, Eneuboulos, and Anementus. After these things was Anodaphus, in the time of Euedoreschus. There were afterwards other kings, and last of all Sisithrus (Xisuthrus). So that, in all, the number amounted to ten kings, and the term of their reigns to one hundred and twenty sari . . .

The account of Apollodorus:

This is the history which Berosus has transmitted to us: He tells us that the first king was Alorus of Babylon, a Chaldaean; he reigned ten sari; and afterwards Alaparus and Amelon, who came from Pantibiblon; then Ammenon the Chaldaean, in whose time appeared the Musarus Oannes, the Annedotus, from the Persian Gulf. (But Alexander Polyhistor, anticipating the event, has said that he appeared in the first year; but Apollodorus says it was after forty sari; Abydenus, however, makes the second Annedotus appear after twenty-six sari.) Then succeeded Megalarus, from the city of Pantibiblon, and he reigned eighteen sari; and after him Daonus, the shepherd, from Pantibiblon, reigned ten sari; in his time (he says) appeared again, from the Persian Gulf, a fourth Annedotus, having the same form with those above, the shape of a fish blended with that of a man. Then Euedoreschus reigned from the city of Pentibiblon for the period of eighteen sari. In his day there appeared another personage, whose name was Odacon, from the Persian Gulf, like the former, having the same complicated form, between a fish and a man. (All these, says Apollodorus, related particularly and circumstantially whatever Oannes had informed them of Concerning these appearances Abydenus has made no mention.) Then Amempsinus, a Chaldaean from Laranchae reigned, and he, being the eighth in order, ruled for ten sari. Then Otiartes, a Chaldaean from Laranchae, reigned, and he ruled for eight sari.

Upon the death of Otiartes, his son Xisuthrus, reigned eighteen sari. In his time the Great Flood happened.

From the further account of Alexander Polyhistor:
After the death of Ardates, his son, Xisuthrus, succeeded, and reigned eighteen sari. In his time happened the great Deluge; the history of which is given in this manner. The deity Kronus appeared to him in a vision, and gave him notice, that upon the fifteenth day of the month Daesia there would be a flood, by which mankind would be destroyed. He therefore enjoined him to commit to writing a history of the beginning, progress, and final conclusion of all things, down to the present term; and to bury these accounts securely in the City of the Sun at Sippara; and to build a vessel, and to take with him into it his friends and relations; and to convey on board everything necessary to sustain life, and to take in also all species of animals that either fly, or rove upon the earth; and trust himself to the deep. Having asked the deity whither he was to sail, he was answered, 'To the Gods' . . .

Interestingly enough, there seems to be no symbolism or esoteric meaning here. It is simply stated, by the Sumerians' descendants, that their civilisation (which, of course, was one of the very earliest on Earth) was founded by non-human creatures.

The strange beings, Oannes, Anndotus, Euedocus, Eneugamus, Eneuboulos, and Anementus, who came out of the Persian Gulf, were amphibious. They would appear only in the daytime, re-

107

turning each night to their aquatic habitat. They seemed to have but one purpose: to instruct man in the ways of civilised life. The arts and sciences and every form of practical knowledge that the Sumerians had were said to have been from the teachings of these creatures, who were half-fish and half-men.

According to the legend, they were endowed with superior knowledge and reason, and were regarded as teachers, but not as gods. They were never called gods, but rather 'animals', 'semi-daemons', and 'personages'. Whatever they were, the Sumerians, in their literature, credited them with the colonisation of the world as they knew it.

On the other hand, we must be cautious, especially in this case, as we are not even dealing with a Sumerian cuneiform inscription, but rather a legend written down in Hellenistic (or later) times, by Greek historians who lived thousands of years after the alleged events. The Oannes legend is almost surely a garbled version of a cosmogony which may or may not have been Sumerian, much less a reliable account of an extraterrestrial contact.

Sagan once mentioned that another ancient account, *The Book of the Secrets of Enoch* (one of the Pseudepigrapha), might also represent a genuine contact myth.[4] The original suggestion, made in 1960, actually came from two Soviet writers, Valentin Rich and Mikhail Chernenkov, and was first published in the Russian *Literary Gazette*.* They thought that Enoch's ascension into heaven might just as well be interpreted as a ride in a flying saucer.

It began in a dream. There appeared two men (angels) whose 'faces were shining like the sun, their eyes . . . like a burning light, and from their lips was fire coming forth with clothing and singing of various kinds in appearance purple, their wings were brighter than gold, their hands whiter than snow.' The two angels said to Enoch: 'the Eternal Lord hath sent thee, and lo! thou shalt today ascend with us into heaven.'

Enoch told how 'the angels took him on to their wings and bore him up on to the first heaven and placed him on the clouds.'[5] A progression, all the way through the tenth heaven, finally

Time magazine, 22 February 1960.

brought Enoch face-to-face with God. Here, the secrets of God were revealed, again (as in the Oannes legend), for the purpose of instructing mankind.

It might be interesting to note here the criteria that Shklovskii and Sagan believe should be satisfied to establish a contact myth as genuine; that is, for it to have a high probability of being connected with extraterrestrial beings. The first three are from their book *Intelligent Life in the Universe*:

[1] . . . we require more of a legend than the apparition of a strange being who does extraordinary works and lives in the sky. It would certainly add credibility if no obvious supernatural adumbration were attached to the story. The legend should not be . . . moulded into [one of] several different standardized supernatural frameworks . . .

[2] A description of the morphology of an intelligent non-human, a clear account of astronomical realities which a primitive people could not acquire by their own efforts . . .

[3] . . . a transparent presentation of the purpose of the contact would increase the credibility of the legend.[6]

More recently, Sagan has added two more points in his book *The Cosmic Connection* (1973):

[4] When information is contained in the legend that could not possibly have been generated by the civilization that created the legend . . .

[5] If an artifact of technology were passed on from an ancient civilisation – an artifact that is far beyond the technological capabilities of the originating civilization – we would have an interesting *prima facie* case for extraterrestrial visitation.[7]

Von Däniken seems to agree, generally, that these are acceptable criteria to use. What is *not* agreed upon – between proponents and debunkers of ancient astronauts – is whether or not any such criteria have ever been fulfilled. Although Sagan, for example, was willing to give serious consideration to the Oannes legend as a *possible* extraterrestrial contact, he was certainly *not* saying that it should be considered as actual 'evidence', much less 'proof', that such an event had occurred.

Of the *Book of Enoch*, Sagan wrote that it 'fails to satisfy several of the criteria for a general contact myth, mentioned above: it has been moulded into several different standardised supernatural frameworks; the astronomy is largely incorrect; and there is no transparent extraterrestial motivation for the events described.'[8]

In *Chariots of the Gods?* von Däniken presents his own version (in more ways than one) of the Gilgamesh Epic (the standard version of which is dated to around 650 BC, but goes back to earlier stories about the figure of Gilgamesh), which he would like us to examine 'in the light of present-day knowledge'.[9]

He tells us that 'the main thread of the Epic of Gilgamesh runs parallel to the biblical book of Genesis'; that 'the narrative contains the idea of interbreeding between "god" and man'; that there are references to a strange creature, Enkidu, 'created by the goddess of heaven, Aruru'; that there is an 'eye-witness account of a space trip'; and that Enkidu suffers from a 'mysterious disease' caused by 'the poisonous breath of a heavenly beast'.[10]

At least, this time, we do have a legend, inscribed on clay tablets in cuneiform script, which is of Akkadian origin, and which has been directly translated from the original tablets (eleven of them in all; the twelfth was attached from another Gilgamesh story, but is not part of the Epic), all found at Nineveh, once the capital of the Assyrian empire (see illus 75). Furthermore, this mythological tale is apparently based on a real personage (to whom the various myths and legends have been attached), a Sumerian king, named Gilgamesh, who reigned during the First Dynasty of Uruk (*c* 2700 BC).

According to the legend, his parents were the goddess Ninsun and a mortal, the high priest of Kullab, making Gilgamesh a demi-god (ie part god and part man). There is nothing to indicate, however, that Ninsun was an extraterrestrial. Most of the other events, cited by von Däniken, are *not* contained in the Gilgamesh epic! To begin with, the main thread of the legend does *not* run parallel to Genesis; only in the eleventh tablet, when the Flood story is related, which is only a small part of the poem, can one recognise a common Near Eastern theme that was also expressed in Genesis. The Epic of Gilgamesh is about man's search for the meaning of life, the inevitability of death, his futile quest for physical immortality, and his acceptance of the philosophy that the only human immortality lay in doing great deeds.

Enkidu, a man-like creature whose whole body was covered with hair, the protector of wild animals, was created by the 'mother goddess', Aruru, to divert the attention of the oppressive ruler Gilgamesh away from the town of Uruk. After a series of events, however, the two adversaries become friends, with Enkidu as the follower and helpful companion of Gilgamesh.

There is no space voyage referred to at all, throughout the eleven tablets of the Epic (nor in Tablet XII). Gilgamesh and Enkidu journey to the 'cedar forest' (in Tablets IV and V), where they kill an ogre by the name of Huwawa; and, after Enkidu's death, Gilgamesh searches to the limits of the world for the secret of immortality. There is absolutely nothing mentioned anywhere in the Epic of Gilgamesh about Enkidu's supposed flight, 'held in the brazen talons of an eagle'[11] and his description (supplied by von Däniken) of how the Earth looked from a great height.

The circumstances of Enkidu's death are likewise wrong in von Däniken's version of the tale. It was decreed by the gods that he should die, after he killed the 'bull of heaven'. There is *no* reference whatever to a 'mysterious disease' nor to the 'poisonous breath of a heavenly beast'. There is no mention of a weight on Enkidu's body 'like the weight of a boulder'[12] which von Däniken likens to the G-forces experienced by astronauts at take-off.

It is one thing to analyse and interpret a genuine myth, for what it is, in the original form; another to find a myth or legend that has been garbled by later Greek historians; and still another matter to have the legend distorted and misrepresented by modern authors who are as careless as von Däniken.

SOURCE NOTES
1 Harold T. Wilkins, *Flying Saucers on the Attack* (New York: Citadel Press, 1954), pp165–76.

2 von Däniken, *In Search of Ancient Gods*, p4.
3 I. S. Shklovskii and Carl Sagan, *Intelligent Life in the Universe* (San Francisco: Holden-Day, 1966), p461.
4 Walter Sullivan, *We Are Not Alone* (New York: McGraw-Hill, 1964), p240.
5 R. H. Charles, ed., *The Apocrypha and Pseudepigrapha of the Old Testament* (London. Oxford University Press, 1913), pp431–2.
6 Shklovskii and Sagan, p454.
7 Carl Sagan, *The Cosmic Connection* (Garden City, New York: Anchor Press/Doubleday & Co., 1973), p205.
8 Shklovskii and Sagan, p454.
9 *Chariots of the Gods?* p69.
10 Ibid., pp64–7.
11 Ibid., p66.
12 Ibid., p65. For a complete English translation of the twelve tablets (with commentary) see: Alexander Heidel, *The Gilgamesh Epic and Old Testament Parallels* (Chicago and London: Phoenix Books/University of Chicago Press, 1946).

*

The Oannes legend has turned up again recently, this time in connection with a new 'mystery', which von Däniken regards as 'conclusive proof . . . of ancient astronauts'.* This tantalising puzzle, which gives the Oannes legend a new twist by placing it in West Africa, was developed in a book called *The Sirius Mystery* (1976), written by an American living in England, Robert K. G. Temple. An orientalist by academic training, Temple claims that ancient knowledge of the Sirius binary system can be traced back over a 5,000-year period to early Greece, Egypt, and Babylonia.

The Sirius Mystery concerns the Dogon peoples, who live in the Republic of Mali, part of the African Sahel region, and their astounding astronomical knowledge, which Temple thinks is best explained as an extraterrestrial contact. The Dogon, who according to some definitions constitute a 'primitive' tribe, reportedly know: (1) that the star Sirius has an invisible companion (ie invisible to the naked eye), a star which the Dogon call *po tolo* (or *Digitaria*), which astronomers nowadays call Sirius B (see illus 76); (2) that this star revolves around Sirius in an elliptical orbit; (3) that it is very small and super-dense (Sirius B is actually a 'white dwarf', and does in fact have these characteristics); and (4) that its orbital period is 50 Earth-years (which is correct).

If true, such extraordinary knowledge possessed by a 'primitive'

*According to a statement he made at the Ancient Astronaut Society meeting held on 13 March 1976, in Chicago, Illinois, USA.

people would seem to satisfy one or more of Sagan and Shklovskii's criteria for a genuine contact 'myth'. The mystery is all the more intriguing in light of Dogon mythology which, according to Temple, includes a story about amphibious creatures (remember Oannes and company – see illus 77) that landed in an 'ark', which raised a 'whirlwind' of dust and 'spurted blood' – interpreted by Temple as 'rocket exhaust'. The leader of the amphibians was called *Nommo*, who resembled 'a kind of cross between a man and a dolphin'.[1] After all, dolphins are known to be intelligent, so this should not surprise us. According to Temple, *Nommo* must have been the one who gave the Dogon their knowledge of Sirius B.

The real clincher for the ancient-astronaut theorists, however, is that this particular knowledge of the Sirius system, which *apparently* has been known by Dogon priests for untold centuries, was not even predicted by European astronomers until 1844, and not actually observed through a telescope until 1862 (first seen by lens-maker Alvan G. Clark through an 18-inch refractor). Hence, how do we account for such an oddity as the Dogon having such information without the benefit of a powerful telescope, much less a working knowledge of astrophysics? Furthermore, as if all this were not enough, the Dogon even worship the invisible companion of Sirius, as evidenced by their *Sigui* feast held every *sixty* years (*not fifty* as might be expected in order for it to coincide with the 50-year orbit of Sirius B), a practice that has reportedly gone on for several hundred years.

But despite what in this case *appears* to be very impressive evidence for an extraterrestrial contact, that evidence does not rest on a very solid foundation. Actually, the deeper one looks into the 'Sirius mystery', the less mysterious it becomes. Again, as in countless other examples of alleged 'evidence' for ancient astronauts, certain key information has been withheld, or missed, by the author writing the story.

In this case, the first 'missing pieces' came to me by way of my friend Richard Greenwell, who is affiliated with the Office of Arid Lands Studies at the University of Arizona, in Tucson. In 1976, Greenwell had co-edited a book entitled *The Application of Technology in Developing Countries*, and he directed my atten-

tion to one particular chapter, by his colleague Dr Hans Guggenheim, an anthropologist. At first glance, the relevance of the
chapter, entitled 'Dual Technological Systems in Water and
Grain Storage', seemed remote from the subject at hand. However, further examination revealed Guggenheim's own experiences
in working with the Dogon, giving them technical assistance, particularly related to water and grain storage techniques. Most
significant of all were the parts concerning historical background,
traditional mythology, and modern-day beliefs and practices
of the Dogon. I would now like to quote *verbatim* from Guggenheim's chapter:

The Dogon began to move into the Bandiagara Plateau, where
they now live, some time between the 13th and the 16th centuries. The area, now the 5th Region of Mali, consists of a huge
flat plain that extends into Upper Volta, of long drawn-out
cliffs of about 500 kilometres in range and about 300 metres in
height, and of a plateau that declines gradually towards the
Niger River. When the Dogon arrived, they were a warring
tribe, proud of their horses and military prowess. They found
an indigenous population, the so-called Tellem. These people
were hunters, but also cultivated the fonio grain. This grain was
cultivated without the need of iron tools, since fonio requires no
labor. The Dogon, however, introduced a more powerful
subsistence crop of millet, together with the art of iron-
working.
   This historical change of diet is documented both in myth
and present consumption habits. The fonio grain is associated
with the creation of the Universe; millet is associated with the
coming of technology. The Dogon perceived enormous energy
concentrated inside a single grain. They believed the fonio
grain to have been the heaviest and smallest element in the Universe, which concentrated within itself enough energy to have
caused the creation of the Universe, as it exploded in a spiraling
arc. Associated with the energy of grain, they see water and
fire. The first is life-giving; the second linked to death, as well
as to human and artistic creativity. The first, water, is the
energy of nature. The second, fire, is seen as the energy of

culture. The seven kinds of millet were brought down to Earth by the heavenly water spirit called *Nommo*. On the occasion of his descent, he stood on a granary, and so once again the concepts of technology, energy, and energy-storage are associated.

The free environment, the plain, the cliffs, and the plateau have offered different opportunities to the Dogon farmers, but have always presented the same problem: lack of water. The soil of the plains is composed of poor sandstone rocks, which permit only a few wells and hamper water research. On the cliffs, water can sometimes be found in small gorges, where runoff accumulates, but the inhabitants of isolated villages sometimes have to walk for as long as three hours in order to find drinking water. The region is part of the Sahel, and its annual precipitation is characterised by extreme variation, ranging from 300 to 600 mm. The Sahelian farmers distinguish these three important seasons: the rainy period, which can begin as early as June and last until September or October; the cool season, that goes from October to February; and the dry season, which covers the rest of the year, except for January showers. The contrast between these seasons is dramatic. A dry and parched land of sand and rock is transformed into a green paradise with rivers and lakes during the summer months, but then reverts to its desolate condition. The uncertainty created by the oscillation between years of drought and rain, as well as for the insecurity of rainfall in a given year, makes planning for the future a necessity. For example, 1976 was a year of relatively high rainfall, but most of the Dogon region experienced a lack of rain during late August, and rain dances asking the rain gods for help were held throughout the area. This mini-drought came at a crucial period in the development of millet, when the grain was in flower. Irrespective of the size of the plant or the length of time it takes for millet to mature, the period between the beginning of flowering and the maturation of the head is always 31 days. Lack of water during this period can effectively destroy a crop, no matter how much it rains before or after. But in 1976, difficulties for the farmer did not end with the dry spell. In October, during the harvest,

116

there were unusual late rains and heavy hailstorms. The latter smashed the millet to the ground. What had promised to be a good harvest turned into a near disaster.

The uncertainty of rain has helped shape the farming practices of the Dogon, and has become the basis for his emphasis on storage as a reduction of risk. It has also provided the basic underlying thoughts of his philosophy and art. For the Dogon, the Universe is engaged in a never-ending struggle between the forces of rain and life, personified by the normal, and the forces of drought and death, represented by the rebel spirit, *the fox*. All elements of nature, society, and language, are classified as belonging to one or to the other. Such pairs include, for example, light and dark, male and female, reason and intuition, paternal family and maternal family, right and left, sheep and goat, etc. Millet, for example, has to be sorted out prior to sowing because some of it is male and grows wild among the rest. The good millet, in contrast, is considered female. Water is classified as good water (the water of rain), belonging to the normal, and as black water, evil water, that brings sickness and disease and rests in puddles in the rocks, which belong to the fox.

For the Dogon farmer, then, security in a world of conflicting forces involves the reduction of risk. One form of this reduction is the emphasis on storage. Storage of grain and storage of water. At the same time Dogon culture is fascinated with the unknown, with change, with agriculture and with technology. 'We will try anything,' a Dogon chief once told me. 'Bring us new seeds or a new tool, or a new solution to a problem, and we will try it.'[2]

Now, a reminder of how the Egyptians depended so heavily on Sirius to tell them when to expect the inundation of the Nile, which was in turn responsible for their major food supply. More specifically, they watched for the first dawn-rising (which astonomers now call the helical rising, meaning 'with the sun') of the Dog star, which during one period also happened to coincide roughly with the summer solstice (around 21 June) and the beginning of the rainy season which would flood the Nile, making the grain crops grow. So, not only did the Egyptians establish a tropical calendar to predict the seasons, based on Sirius, but great religious significance was attached, as well, to this seemingly life-giving star. The whole agricultural cycle that was first signalled by this brightest of all stars in the night (or pre-dawn) sky clearly dominated Egyptian life.

Upon checking the location of Mali, where the Dogon live, relative to Egypt – where Sirius had been so important – one finds that the two countries are not so very far apart and, most important from the standpoint of archaeo-astronomy, they are quite close in latitude, which means that the helical rising of Sirius in Mali occurs near *their* summer solstice, also.

A likely solution to the 'Syrius mystery' now begins to take shape. I strongly suspect that, prior to the 1920s, the Dogon did *not* worship Sirius B, but rather Sirius (or Sirius A), and for good reason, as we have just seen. Furthermore, it is not entirely clear just how 'ancient' the Sigui festival really is. And despite what Temple may wish to believe, the Dogon's knowledge of Sirius B (or Digitaria) has *not* been established prior to 1931. All we have is the word of the Dogon priests, who are already steeped in myth and fantasy of the highest order. One of the Hogon (as the Dogon priests are called) even claimed 'that he had been to Digitaria',[3] which makes him somewhat like a UFO 'contactee'.

Perhaps the Sigui festival is truly ancient, as a ceremony dedicated to the star Sirius, which would seem quite reasonable knowing the true circumstances of the Dogon's agricultural cycle – crucial information that was either ignored or perhaps not known by Temple or von Däniken. Also, the important notion in Dogon mythology that each element of nature is one of a pair of opposites 'primed' them for a suggestion such as an invisible *dark* companion to the *brightest* star Sirius, which, we might suppose, already figured heavily in their agricultural and hence religious life. Imagine, here is a tribe of people *already* believing that the life-giving fonio grain is the heaviest and smallest element in the Universe, and to have caused the creation of the Universe, and *already* worshipping the star Sirius for signalling the impending rains that will nourish the growth of this grain (upon which their life depends); then, information reaches them (during the late 1920s) that 'their star' Sirius has an invisible dark companion that is very small and 'super-heavy'. It would only be natural for them to be excited at the idea, and adopt it as part of their Sirius ritual.

Soon after the discovery of Sirius B, in 1862, astronomers went to work trying to determine just what kind of star it was. They were puzzled by its dim appearance, combined with an apparent large mass (approximately equal to that of our sun) sufficient to cause the perturbations observed in Sirius. They were astonished at the spectrographic results which indicated a very hot, dim, and small star, which theoretically would have a radius a hundred times smaller, and a mean density of a million times greater, than the sun.

In an article entitled 'Sirius Enigmas' (*Technology Review*, December 1977), MIT (Massachusetts Institute of Technology) physicist Dr Kenneth Brecher wrote:

Sir Arthur Eddington's popular books on astronomy, written in the late 1920s, confirm that nobody believed there could be anything in the universe anywhere near so dense. I have found references in the 1920s to Sirius B in *Le Monde*, *The New York Times*, and *Scientific American*. It was the black hole of its day . . .

A[n] . . . obvious possibility is that somebody told the Dogon all about Sirius before Griaule and Dieterlen ever arrived. The sequence of events, as imagined independently by Carl Sagan, Ian Roxborough, and myself, might run as follows. As I've tried to emphasise, Sirius B was important and widely disseminated news in the 1920s. Some Jesuit priest reads about it in *Le Monde*, and then goes to Mali long before Griuale and Dieterlen.

'Tell us your myths,' say the Dogon.

'Do you see that star?' replies the priest; 'it is actually two stars, and the invisible star is the heaviest thing there is.'

The Dogon promptly incorporate this information into their culture. And when the two anthropologists are told the secrets of the Dogon, all they get is a cross-cultural translation.

Now it seems to me that this is no doubt the most likely explanation for the knowledge possessed by the tribe.

Furthermore, the source of the information need not have been someone visiting the area. In fact, it would seem just as likely that a Dogon student attending one of the nearby schools picked up this titbit (along with others to be discussed shortly) and took it back home. Despite the impression created by Temple that the Dogon are an isolated culture, such is not the case (nor has it been for several centuries). Von Däniken even quotes, in his latest book, *According to the Evidence* (1978), the statement of Professor Michael Ovenden (Professor of Astronomy at the University of Vancouver, Canada), published originally in *Nature* (Vol 261, 17 June 1976): 'In order to understand the survival of ancient traditions among the Dogon, we have only to remember that the leading Moslem university was flourishing at Timbuctu in Mali during the sixteenth century. The traditions of the Greeks, Egyptians and Sumerians flowed through Timbuctu.' Two American astronomers, Peter Pesch (of the Warner and Swasey Observatory, Case Western Reserve University) and Roland Pesch (of Oberlin College), in an article for *The Observatory*, have this to say:

. . . we would like to point out that the unwary reader might, on reading Griaule and Dieterlen come away with the impression that the Dogon, living in a remote part of Africa, had had little or no contact with European culture prior to their field work (carried out in the 1940s). This is simply not the case. There have been French schools, which included 'geography and natural history' in their curricula in the area since 1907. There are also Islamic schools and those Dogon who wish to pursue higher or technical studies in the French system can do and have done so in nearby towns. Dogon culture has shown itself to be very resilient in its response to acculturation; it has quite successfully and completely incorporated aspects of Islamic ritual and culture into its own cultural structure. It may well have incorporated more than that: no culture exists in a vacuum, and most certainly not Dogon culture. The researcher who may find clear evidence of astronomical knowledge of the sort Temple claims for the Dogon might do well, in seeking to explain it, to consider the most likely source of that knowledge – our own culture – before suggesting mystical sources or going back several thousand years and inferentially adding it, together with the Secret of the Great Pyramid and interstellar beacons, to the store of knowledge of storybook Egyptians.[4]

Back in the 1920s, some astronomers thought they had found evidence (some direct visual observations and a perturbation with a period of 6.4 years and an amplitude of about 0.14 seconds of arc) indicating a *third* star in the Sirius system. These speculations were published, and interestingly enough *also* picked up by the Dogon. However, during the period 1965–72, Dr Irving W. Lindenblad, of the US Naval Observatory in Washington, DC, proved the speculations wrong. He reported in *The Astronomical Journal* that: 'The nearly straight arcs described by the residuals in both coordinates over an interval of 6.8 years demonstrate that the 6.4-perturbation, with a total amplitude of 0'.14, does not exist. There is no astronomic evidence, therefore, of a close companion to either Sirius A or Sirius B.'[5]

The oldest documented account of the Dogon's knowledge of Sirius is contained in the article entitled 'A Sudanese Sirius System', written by two French anthropologists, M. Griaule and G. Dieterlen, first published in 1950. Claims of any earlier knowledge of Sirius B among the Dogon rest entirely on Temple's interpretations, which are highly arbitrary and ambiguous, to say the least. *The Sirius Mystery* contains some two hundred pages of what I would describe as groping and arbitrary 'identifications' of supposed connections between the Dogon's knowledge of the Sirius system and references – each taken out of its original context – contained in such stories as the Epic of Gilgamesh, Jason and the Argonauts, tales of Hercules, and others. Temple's so-called 'tracing back' through five thousand years of history does not constitute a coherent pattern at all, and the 'references' he finds to support ancient knowledge of the Sirius system are so strained and arbitrary, they become meaningless.

For example, because Hercules is said to have slept with fifty women in one night, we are supposed to connect this reference up with the fifty-year orbital period of Sirius B! Likewise, the reference to Jason and his fifty argonauts and a mythical hound with fifty heads (because Sirius was also known as the 'Dog Star'). Temple thinks he sees cryptic hints of Sirius B anywhere and everywhere, and produces a random patchwork of word-games (ie linguistic 'identifications', most of which constitute a play on words) and supposed connections that he force-fits into his preconceived theory. The whole process is clearly a rationalisation, *ad hoc*, made to support a conclusion decided upon in advance.

Temple has also distorted much of the cosmogony and cosmology that Griaule and Dieterlen have passed on to us. Several key elements (which pertain to Temple's argument) of the Nommo legend appear differently in the book *African Worlds* (in a chapter on the Dogon by Griaule and Dieterlen), a source that Temple cites, than in Chapter Eight (entitled 'A Fable') of *The Sirius Mystery*.

Whereas Temple speaks of an '*ark* [italics mine] in which the Nommos [ie ancient astronauts] actually landed on earth'[6], Griaule and Dieterlen say that Nommo 'came down to earth *on a gigantic arch* [italics mine], at the centre of which stood the two *Nommo* of the sky',[7] and that 'He manifests himself in the rainbow, which is called "the path of the Nommo".'[8] The Nommo (in the plural) are also credited, in the Dogon creation myth (as told to the two anthropologists), as 'creators of the sky and the stars'[9] (quite an accomplishment for mere space travellers). (And, of course, the stars would have had to exist already, before any intelligent beings could develop around them; an obvious inconsistency that apparently does not bother Temple.) One of the Nommo even brought with him a fragment of his placental egg which became the Earth.[10]

Although somewhat abstruse, another bit of Dogon cosmogony is quite revealing:

The . . . primordial movements are conceived in terms of an ovoid form – 'the egg of the world' (*aduno tal*) – within which lie, already differentiated, the germs of things; in consequence of the spiral movement of extension the germs develop first in seven segments of increasing length, representing the seven fundamental seeds of cultivation, which are to be found again in the human body, and which, with the *Digitaria*, indicate the predominance of the Ogdoad or Divine Octet in this system of thought: the organisation of the cosmos, of man, and of society. At the seventh vibration the segment breaks its envelope. This segment is the symbol of the seed which plays a primary role in the life and thought of the Dogon – the *emme ya*, female sorghum, which represents life, and ideal food, immune from impurity.

Having broken its wrapping the creative process emerges to follow the predestined and predetermined movement of being. For inside the first seed, and forming its central core, was an oblong plate divided into four sectors in which lay the signs corresponding to the twenty-two categories into which the universe is classified, each placed under the direction of one of the four elements: air, fire, earth, and water. In the rotatory movement of creation this plate, turning itself, flings off the signs into space, where they come to rest, each one on the things which it symbolises and which till then existed only potentially. At their touch every being comes into existence and is automatically placed in the predetermined category.

All these images seem to relate to an effort of discovery, an attempt to apprehend the infinitely small at its point of departure towards the immeasurably vast. *In fact, the order of the heavens, as it is observed and conceived by the Dogon, is no more than a projection, infinitely expanded, of events and phenomena which occur in the infinitely small* [italics mine].

The starting-point of creation is the star which revolves round Sirius and is actually named the '*Digitaria* star': it is regarded by the Dogon as the smallest and the heaviest of all the stars; it contains the germs of all things. Its movement on its own axis and around Sirius upholds all creation in space.[11]

The reader now has more of the complete context from which Temple has plucked the supposed 'mystery', and it is certainly obvious how adaptable the discovery of Sirius **B** – the *Digitaria* star – would be (and probably *was*) in this conceptual framework.

On page 43 of *The Sirius Mystery*, Temple reproduces a Dogon drawing of the first seven vibrations, ie 'the spiral of creation', but, *without* an important feature that *does* appear with an otherwise similar drawing in *African Worlds* – namely, 'the egg of the world'.[12] It happens that this particular feature is the so-called 'ellipse' (so designated by Temple, but never by the Dogon) that encloses the Dogon sand drawing of the Sirius system. As pointed out by the science writer Ian Ridpath, in his recent book *Messages From the Stars*, the information that Sirius B orbits Sirius A in an ellipse does *not* come from the Dogon:

> Actually, it comes from Robert Temple. At a yearly ceremony known as the *bado*, the Dogon make a sand drawing of the Sirius system [see illus 78]. This time they place *emme ya*, 'the sun of women', at the centre. Around it are marked Sirius, represented by a cross; Digitaria, shown in two positions, drawn as a horseshoe shape to indicate its nature as a collector and distributor of matter placed in it by the Creator; and five other signs representing different objects, one of them the Nommo. Drawn around these symbols is an oval, the egg of the world. The oval is a device which the Dogon use to enclose other diagrams, not just of Sirius.[13]

Temple has also omitted the fact that the Dogon have an elaborate cosmological system which includes much more astronomy (or rather astrology) than the mere references to one star, Sirius B. In one of Griaule and Dieterlen's other publications, a book entitled *L'Homme: Signes Graphiques Soudanais* (1951), they tell about several groups of constellations and specific celestial bodies other than Sirius, that are likewise important to the Dogon. Figuring heavily in this cosmological system are the bright planets Venus and Jupiter, the north star Polaris, and the Pleiades star cluster. And, as we might expect, the Dogon decorate their sanctuaries with signs of the constellations representing the different (planting) seasons of the year.

Now, for the most crucial test of all, of a possible extraterrestrial contact with the Dogon; we must ask the question: *does the special knowledge of the Dogon represent Earthbound astronomy or extraterrestrial science?* I think the answer to this question is quite clear. The astronomical knowledge of the Dogon that we are told about in Temple's book has all the tell-tale signs of Earth-based information (which has since been revised) and is *typical* of the first things learned by the novice in astronomy. When I first took up the hobby of astronomy at the age of twelve, the first things I would show my friends and relatives through my new 3-inch telescope were the four Galilean moons of Jupiter and Saturn's rings. Those are precisely the other extraterrestrial titbits, Temple reports, that the Dogon know. Of course, we now know better: Jupiter has at least fourteen satellites at last count, and, more relevant to the question of Sirius B, white dwarf stars are no longer believed to be the smallest and heaviest bodies in the universe. Rapidly rotating neutron stars called pulsars (about 100 million times as dense) and the incredible 'black holes' are the new candidates for such honours. Had some super-intelligent inter-stellar explorers been involved, we would surely expect their astronomical knowledge to be somewhat more advanced that it appears to be.

SOURCE NOTES

1 Robert K. G. Temple, *The Sirius Mystery* (London: Sidgwick & Jackson, 1976), pp207, 211–12.

2 Robert L. Bulfin, Jr. and J. Richard Greenwell, eds., *The Application of Technology in Developing Countries* (Tucson, Arizona: The University of Arizona, Office of Arid Lands Studies, 1977), pp25–6.

3 Temple, p42.

4 Peter Pesch and Roland Pesch, 'The Dogon and Sirius', in *The Observatory*, Vol 97, No 1016, pp27–8.

5 Irving W. Lindenblad, 'Multiplicity of the Sirius System', in *The Astronomical Journal*, Vol 78, No 2, March 1973, p207.

6 Temple, p213.

7 Marcel Griaule and Germaine Dieterlen, 'The Dogon', in *African Worlds*, edited by Daryll Forde (London: Oxford University Press, 1954), p86.

8 Temple, p215.
9 Griaule and Dieterlen, p86.
10 Ibid., p86.
11 Ibid., pp84–5.
12 Ibid., p84.
13 Ian Ridpath, *Messages From the Stars* (New York: Harper & Row, 1978), p182.

13 EXO-THEOLOGY: THE RELIGION OF OUTER SPACE

Carl Gustav Jung, world-famous psychoanalyst (and philosopher-psychologist), is best known, perhaps, for some of the terms he coined such as 'complex', 'introvert', and 'extrovert' but he made his mark in UFO research as well. His little book, *Flying Saucers – A Modern Myth of Things Seen in the Skies* (1958), has had a lasting influence on virtually every ufologist who has ever considered the psychological and sociological aspects of the UFO phenomenon.

Dr Jung was born in Kesswil, Thurgau, Switzerland, on 26 July 1875, and died at Kusnacht, Zurich, on 6 June 1961. He earned his medical degree (Doctor of Medicine) from the University of Basle, in 1900, and took a position, shortly thereafter, at the University of Zurich Psychiatric Clinic. His collaboration with Sigmund Freud lasted from 1907 to 1914; Jung then established his own school of thought, called Analytical Psychology (later renamed 'Complex Psychology'). The year 1921 saw the publication of Jung's classic book, *Psychological Types*, wherein the terms 'introvert' and 'extrovert' were first introduced.

According to Jungian theory, the human psyche is embroiled in a battle of 'opposites' as he called them: extroversion *versus* introversion; the *ego* (centre of the conscious self) *versus* the *persona* (our social mask); the *persona versus* the *shadow* (unconscious natural self); thinking and feeling (rational functions) *versus* sensation and intuition (irrational forces); etc. The dominant component is that which determines the individual's psychological type. Making matters more complex are the archetypes or 'primordial images', superimposed, as it were, in both personal and collective layers. The archetypes are manifested symbolically in myths, dreams, and psychoses. Certain of these symbols are common to every human psyche as part of what Jung called the 'collective unconscious'. He once said, 'The archetypes of the unconscious can be shown empirically to be the equivalents of religious dogmas.' Examples are the 'old wise man', the 'great mother' and the mandala (a Sanskrit word meaning 'magic circle') which Jung thought of as representing UFOs.

It is one of the oldest religious symbols, found throughout the world. Frieda Fordham wrote, in her biography of Jung, *An Introduction to Jung's Psychology* (1953):

Historically, the mandala served as a symbol representing the nature of the deity, both in order to clarify it philosophically, and for the purpose of adoration. Jung found the mandala symbolism occurring spontaneously in the dreams and visions of many of his patients. Its appearance was incomprehensible to them, but it was usually accompanied by a strong feeling of harmony or of peace.[1]

Jung himself later wrote (in *Flying Saucers – A Modern Myth*):

In so far as the mandala encompasses, protects, and defends the psychic totality against outside influences and seeks to unite the inner opposites, it is at the same time a distinct *individuation symbol* and was known as such even to medieval alchemy. The soul was supposed to have the form of a sphere, on the analogy of Plato's world-soul, and we meet the same symbol in modern dreams, By reason of its antiquity, this symbol leads us to the heavenly spheres, to Plato's 'supra-celestial place', where the 'Ideas' of all things are stored up. Hence there would be nothing against the naïve interpretation of the UFOs as 'souls'. Naturally they do not represent our modern conception of the soul, but rather an involuntary archetypal or mythological conception of an unconscious content, a *rotundum*, as the alchemists called it, that expresses the totality of the individual ...

128

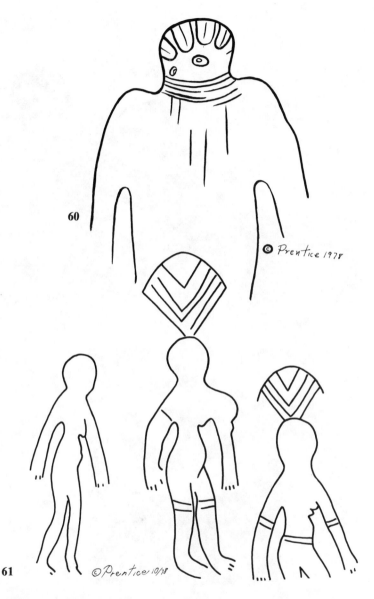

60. Jabbaren, the 'Great Martian God'. Drawing by Diane Prentice.

61. Tassili frescoes thought by von Däniken to represent 'astronauts' with 'antennae' on their 'helmets'. Archaeologists more knowledgeable than von Däniken interpret these prehistoric Africans as women with baskets on their heads. *Drawing by Diane Prentice.*

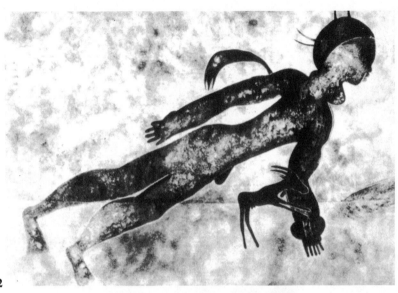

62

63

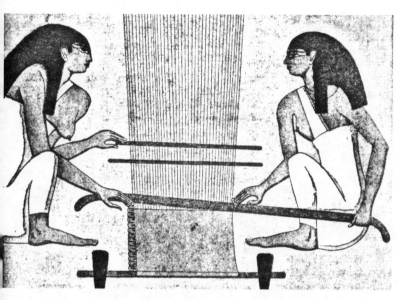

62. Another Tassili painting, interpreted by von Däniken as a being 'wearing a close-fitting space suit with steering gear on his shoulders and antennae on his protective helmet' (see *Return to the Stars,* pictorial section between pp48-49). However, the complete scene, from which the individual has been extracted, shows a confrontation fought with bows and arrows. The French archaeologist, Henri Lhote, the discoverer of this and other Tassili art, thinks that 'space-helmets' are more likely skull caps decorated with feathers.

63. This rock painting from Central Kimberley, Australia, is another one of von Däniken's 'Space-Gods' who supposedly created us *in their image.* But how can hundreds of 'spacemen' from all over the world — all looking different — all be the 'spacemen' who modelled us after them?

64. Two women weaving linen at a horizontal loom. From *History of Egypt,* Vol.2.

65

65. Close-up of a portion of the Piri Re'is map. Note that the ancient astronaut's camera even captured this unicorn standing among clumps of grass!

66. The Piri Re'is map of 1513. Africa is upper right, South America is at lower left, and the southernmost part supposedly represents the coastline of Antarctica. *From the map collection of the University of Arizona Library.*

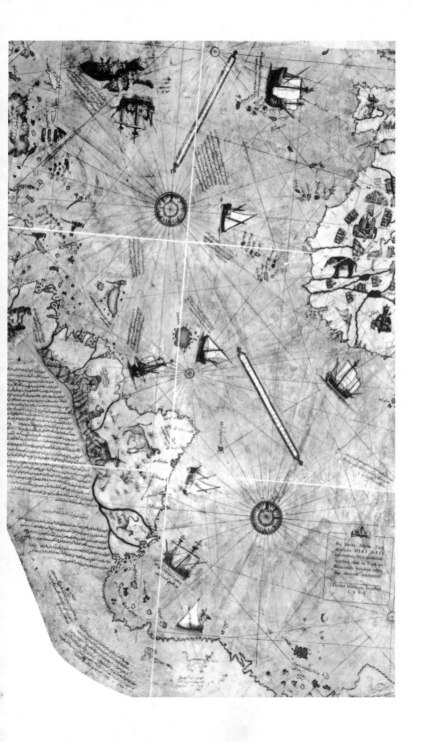

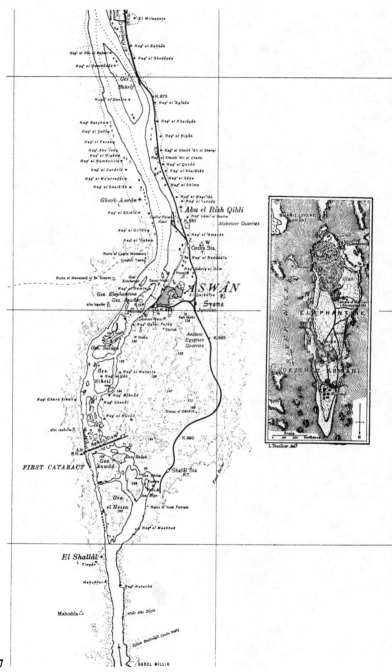

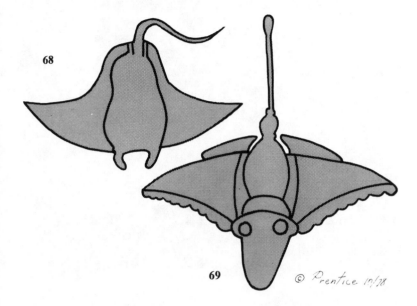

68

69

© Prentice 10/78

67. The Island of Elephantine. From *History of Egypt,* Vol. 2 by G. Maspero (London: The Grolier Society, 1906).
On p. 85 of Chariots of the Gods? (Corgi pb. edition) von Däniken says that 'Every tourist knows the Island of Elephantine . . . the island is called Elephantine even in the oldest texts, because it was supposed to resemble an elephant. The texts were quite right — the island does look like an elephant. But how did the ancient Egyptians know that, because this shape can only be recognized from a very great height?'
   In point of fact, the island was originally called *Yeb* or *Yebu,* in Egyptian, because of the ivory that was sold there; for it has been suggested that elephants did once occupy the place. Similarly, its later name, Elephantine, is derived from the Greek word *elephantinos,* meaning 'ivory'. Furthermore, this tiny island in the Nile is not at all shaped like an elephant, as anyone can see from the accompanying map.

68 and 69. Although von Däniken, and some other proponents of ancient astronauts, prefer to interpret certain Pre-Columbian artifacts like the one depicted on the right as a 'delta-wing jet', there is far more reason to believe that the little gold trinkets are actually stylised representations, both of the Pacific 'flying fish', in some cases, and of the majestic *Manta birostris,* or 'devilfish', in others. The above drawing on the left depicts prominent features of the devilfish for comparison.

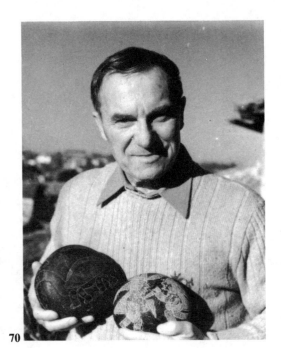

70. Author Robert Charroux holding two of the Cabrera stones.

71. A crater in a marshy region of central Siberia. Photo taken on Kulik expedition.

70

71

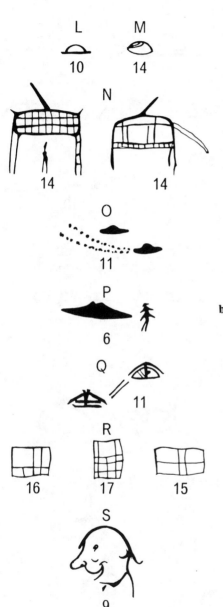

b

72.a. Cave drawings, reprinted from *Flying Saucer Review*.
b. Photograph taken near Yungay, Peru in March 1967. Note the similarity to cave drawing no 11.

73a

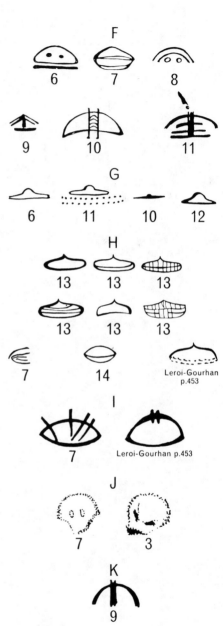

73a. Photograph of a 'flying disc'
taken by Ed Keffel on 7 May
1952 in the vicinity of Barra da
Tijuca, Brazil. Note the similarity
to cave drawing no 10.
b. Cave drawings, reprinted from
Flying Saucer Review.

b

Types of unknown objects portrayed in the
Palaeolithic caves of France and Spain

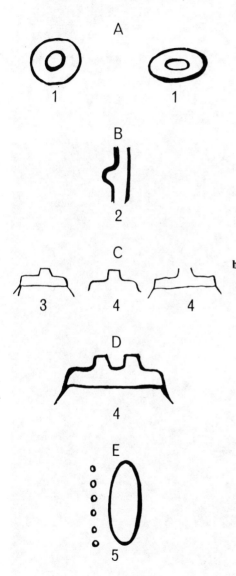

74a. Cave drawings, reprinted
from *Flying Saucer Review*.
b. Another photograph taken
from the same series taken by Ed
Keffel. Note similarity to cave
drawing no. 1.

75

76

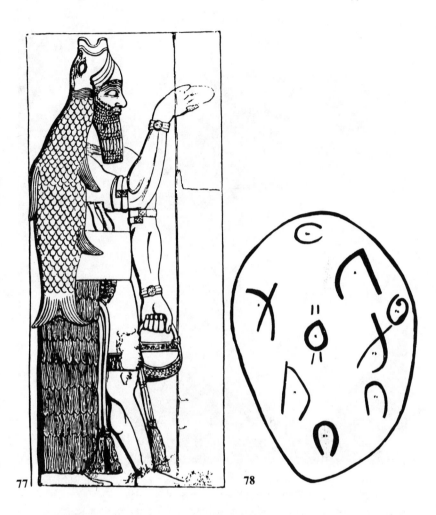

77   78

75. Gilgamesh strangling a lion, flanked by winged human-headed bulls. From *The Book of the Prophet Ezekiel,* by C.H. Toy.

76. The bright star Sirius and its white dwarf companion Sirius B. The six-cusped image of Sirius A and its own multiple 'false' images are due to diffracted light from a special device (a wire grating mounted on an hexagonal diaphram) needed to separate the images of the two stars photographically. The small dot at the lower-right of the main image is Sirius B. *US Naval Observatory Photograph by Dr Irving W. Lindenblad, Washington, DC.*

77. This illustration, wrongly identified by Robert Temple as Oannes, depicts an Assyrian priest.

78. Dogon drawing of the Sirius System. Note that the oval drawn around these symbols is *not* an ellipse, but represents instead the 'egg of the world', as it does on other drawings by the Dogon (after Griaule and Dieterlen).

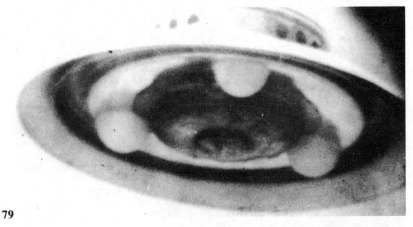

79

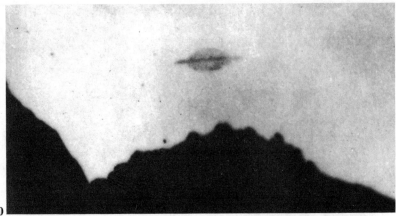

80

79. Venusian 'scout craft' supposedly photographed by George Adamski, which he maintained was similar to the 'wheel within a wheel' that Ezekiel saw.

80-85: Some UFO photographs which most UFOlogists believe are genuine:-

80. Trindade Island, Brazil, 16 January 1958.

81 and 82. McMinnville, Oregon, 11 May 1950.

83. Barra da Tijuca, Brazil, 7 May 1952.

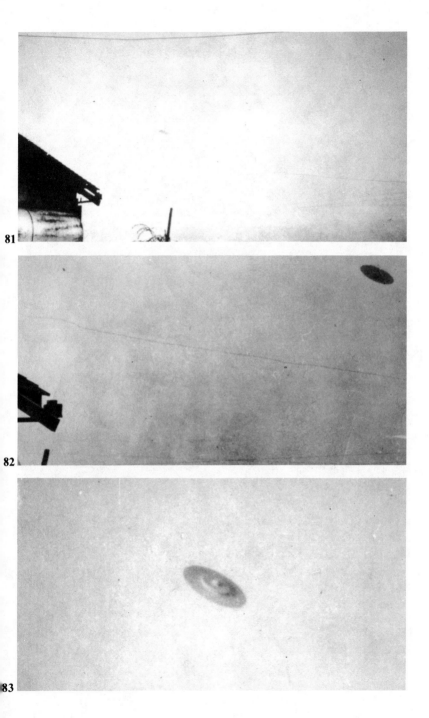

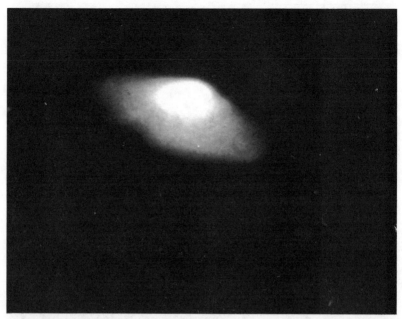

84. Near St George, Minnesota, 21 October 1965.

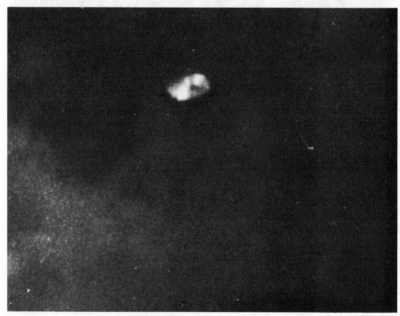

85. Near Yungay, Peru, March 1967.

If the round shining objects that appear in the sky be regarded as visions, we can hardly avoid interpreting them as
archetypal images. They would then be involuntary, automatic
projections based on instinct, and as little as any other psychic
manifestations or symptoms can they be dismissed as meaningless and merely fortuitous.[2]

A matter of clarification should be introduced at this point. Jung
did imply that since thoughts and dreams are *weightless*, as are
UFOs (apparently), UFOs *could be* purely mental and have no
existence outside the mind of the beholder. But, he also moderated
himself on this point by stating that '. . . something is seen, but
one doesn't know what' [italics in the original].[3] He also disquali-
fied himself on the question of the physical reality or non-reality
of UFOs, saying that he would confine his discussion to the
'psychic concomitants' of the UFO phenomenon *only*, leaving
open the question of whether UFOs do or do not exist in the
'physical' realm.[4] His position was simply one of suspended
judgment, while at the same time expounding on the 'visionary
rumour', which is at least a by-product of UFOs, and what it
reveals about the psychic nature of human beings.

Jung noticed that dreams, myths, and religions are means by
which all peoples of the world can cope with conflicts through
wish-fulfilment. Even when things are bad, religious man does
not easily accept the conclusion that his prayers have gone un-
answered. Therefore he invents (unconsciously) the 'gods' he
needs. Throughout human existence, our ancestors have always
had to cope with the 'Four Horseman – death, famine, disease,
and the malice of other men'.[5] Wish-fulfilment – even in the realm
of pure imagination – is a way of coping with a real world that
may be somewhat more harsh than we would like.

The human mind also requires 'psychic balance'. We might
draw a rather crude and oversimplified analogy to the physical
body, which needs the right kind of food, regulating chemicals, all
at the proper temperature, pressure, etc. The human brain and
'mind' has even more delicate regulatory needs, which can be kept
in balance partly in dreams, myths, and religion. Therefore, we
should be acutely aware of our natural propensity to desire

what is needed for our mental regulatory system. One such element is 'humankind's age-old need for wonder, and striving for supernormal companionship in this vast and lonely universe'.[6]

In *Chariots of the Gods?* von Däniken makes this statement: 'People block the road to serious research by boundless stupidity. There are "contact men" who claim to be in communication with extraterrestrial beings . . .'[7] Then in *Miracles of the Gods*, he writes: 'The situation seems clear to me. Extraterrestrial *impulses* cause the brain to produce visions.'[8] In other words, the ancient astronauts are still communicating with us, but now through visions and apparitions that are often 'mistaken' for religious experiences.

> For example, when an angel appears to the eighteen-year-old [*] Joseph Smith, the founder of the Mormon Religion, and says he knows the secret place where tablets with the history of mankind are hidden, and if it then turns out that the tablets are found exactly at the spot described, this means to me that extraterrestrial beings have given Joseph Smith information that could only be known to them. (Because they prepared the hiding place on our planet thousands of years ago!)[9]

Let us not forget von Däniken's own visionary experience when he was nineteen years old, the contents of which he declines to discuss. Yes, von Däniken, in his own way, is a 'contactee' reminiscent of the 'contact men' of the 1950s. The earlier contactees, like von Däniken, provided a central focal point for those who became disenchanted with organised religion, but whose psychological needs were still acute.

One perennial need of humankind has always been to feel a sense of belonging, which religion satisfies by bringing together like-minded people to wonder and worry in unison. Fears of an uncertain future are not nearly so great when one can share those fears with others. The problem of uncertainty is reduced as well. The contactees of the fifties (like von Däniken in the seventies) gave pretentious, but *definite* answers to key questions about the

*This figure is in error. Joseph Smith was actually fourteen years of age at the time of his experience.

nature of God and the meaning of human existence; questions that have perplexed some of the greatest minds on Earth for thousands of years. People who are seeking this kind of starry-eyed gospel can put their minds to rest (quite literally) and worry no longer.

One of the first, and also generally regarded as the most famous of all the contactees was George Adamski (1891–1965). He is described by his disciples (the present-day George Adamski Foundation based in Vista, California) as a (former) author-lecturer on Unidentified Flying Objects, space travel, Cosmic Philosophy, and the Universal Laws of Life. Since I have already given an account of Adamski's first 'contact' with a man from Venus in *The Space-Gods Revealed*, I will concentrate here on his Biblical exegesis, which follows closely that of Erich von Däniken.

Adamski cites many of the standard passages often interpreted as UFOs and contacts with UFO crews, including Genesis 6:2 and 6:4, describing 'sons of God' who 'came in unto the daughters of men, and they bare children to them . . .' Like von Däniken, Adamski agrees that a 'mating' took place between aliens and Earthwomen.

Adamski furthermore interprets the visions of Ezekiel as a space-vehicle, but not as an 'amphibious helicopter' in the manner of von Däniken. It is always interesting to see how different authors, all supporting the notion of ancient astronauts, can derive quite different results from the same basic data (in this case, the same Biblical passages). According to Adamski, Verses 1:15–28 of Ezekiel describe quite clearly the Venusian 'scout ship', in which he, himself, claims to have flown. Verse 1:18 in particular, he says, '. . . describes the high ring around the dome and even goes so far as to describe four portholes. These verses [1:16 and 18] are a very accurate description of the three-ball-landing-gear type of saucer as seen through the eyes of Ezekiel.'[10] (See illus 79.) If one uses the following translation of these verses, from *The Book of the Prophet Ezekiel* edited by Keith W. Carley, I think we must concede that Adamski's interpretation is at least as reasonable as Josef Blumrich's.

Ezekiel (1:16–18): The wheels sparkled like topaz, and they

131

were all alike: in form and working they were like a wheel inside a wheel, and when they moved in any of the four directions they never swerved in their course. All four had hubs and each hub had a projection which had the power of sight, and the rims of the wheels were full of eyes all round.

Ezekiel (1:28): I saw what looked like fire with encircling radiance. Like a rainbow in the clouds on a rainy day was the sight of that encircling radiance; it was like the appearance of the glory of the *Lord*.[11]

Verse 1:28 is interpreted by Adamski as '. . . the many changing colours of the craft's force field . . .'[12] Again, an exegesis just as reasonable (or unreasonable), and just as *arbitrary* as what we get from Blumrich, von Däniken, or any of the other Space-God proponents.

The most profoundly religious of all the major contactees is Orfeo Angelucci, who claimed to have been baptised and 'reborn' on board a flying saucer. His special contribution to saucer history, as might be guessed, is his religious teaching as revealed to him by the Space People.

Angelucci's early childhood was plagued by physical and emotional problems (among them, an ailment diagnosed as 'constitutional inadequacy'), forcing him to quit school while in the ninth grade. At home, young Angelucci spent most of his time studying 'all branches of sciences'.[13]

His first job was with his uncle's flooring and stucco company as an estimator and salesman. Then in 1936, Orfeo met Mabel Borgianni, whom he later married. The Angeluccis had two sons and eventually moved from New Jersey to California, where Orfeo found work as a mechanic with Lockheed Aircraft Corporation in Burbank. But it was back in New Jersey where Angelucci saw his first 'flying saucer'.

It took place on 4 August 1946, during one of Angelucci's 'science' experiments. He wanted to learn what effect the upper atmosphere would have on certain mould cultures that he'd prepared. He planned to find out by sending the culture dishes aloft, utilising several Navy-type balloons, which he had purchased for the occasion. By accident, the balloons broke loose prematurely; and the cultures were lost. But, while watching the balloons sail away, Angelucci caught sight of a round, wingless craft. He would not know its significance until six years later.

His second experience occurred after the move to California. It was one of the most spectacular of all 'contactee' tales. On 23 May 1952, Orfeo was returning from work, after the nightshift, when he noticed a 'faintly red-glowing oval-shaped object' hovering over the horizon ahead of him. The disc 'pulsated violently' and finally 'shot off into the sky at a 30° or 40° angle', disappearing like a meteor. But, before disappearing, the disc dropped off two smaller orbs (each about 3 feet in diameter) of a 'soft fluorescent green' colour, from which a voice was heard: 'Don't be afraid, Orfeo, we are friends.' The voice then requested that Orfeo get out of his car and listen up. He was informed that ever since his first sighting of a flying saucer back in 1946 (during the balloon experiment), 'friends from another world' had been watching him. The voice said, 'Drink from the crystal cup you will find on the fender of your car, Orfeo.' And he did. Angelucci said, 'It was the most delicious beverage I had ever tasted . . . as I was drinking a feeling of strength and well-being swept over me . . .' Suddenly, another strange thing happened.

The twin, pulsating spheres dimmed slightly; and between them (they were about 3 feet apart) something like a luminous three-dimensional screen appeared. On it were the outline-figures of a man and a woman. The images struck Angelucci as the 'ultimate of perfection'. Orfeo seemed to be in telepathic communication with them. He said, 'I had the uncomfortable feeling as they studied me that they knew every thought in my mind; everything I'd ever done and a vast amount about me that I didn't even know myself. Intuitively, I sensed that I stood in a kind of spiritual nakedness before them.' The figures finally faded and the screen vanished. Just then, the two glowing orbs flared up into brilliant green fire. This time the voice delivered a lengthy sermon, a sample of which follows:

The people of your planet have been under observation for centuries, but have only recently been re-surveyed. Every point of progress in your society is registered with us. We know you

133

as you do not know yourselves. Every man, woman and child is recorded in vital statistics by means of our recording crystal discs. Each of you is infinitely more important to us than to your fellow Earthlings because you are not aware of the true mystery of your being . . .

We feel a deep sense of brotherhood towards Earth's inhabitants because of an ancient kinship of our planet with Earth. In you we can look far back in time and recreate certain aspects of our former world. With deep compassion and understanding we have watched your world going through its 'growing pains'. We ask that you look upon us simply as older brothers.

The voice ended with: 'We'll contact you again, Orfeo, but for now, friend, it is goodnight.' The twin discs flared up again, one last time, and went the way of the larger red one, leaving Angelucci bewildered and alone to ponder his future.[14]

Three more 'contact' experiences followed (both in California and back in New Jersey), culminating in a mystical, 'out-of-the-body' experience, lasting for seven days, in which Angelucci's 'soul' was 'transported into heaven'.

Jung felt that Angelucci's case was a classic. According to Jung:

Without having the faintest inkling of psychology, Angelucci had described in the greatest detail the mystic experience associated with a Ufo [sic] vision . . .

. . . Orfeo's book is an essentially naïve production which for that very reason reveals all the more clearly the unconscious background of the Ufo phenomenon and therefore comes like a gift to the psychologist. The individuation process, the central problem of modern psychology, is plainly depicted in it in an unconscious, symbolical form . . . although the author with his somewhat primitive mentality has taken it quite literally as a concrete happening.[15]

Orfeo is, today, alive and well, and living in Los Angeles.

The Grand Master of OSC (outer space communications) was

the late George W. Van Tassel (1910–78) who owned and operated the Giant Rock Airport (and its concessions) near Yucca
Valley, California, where annual 'space conventions' (actually
gatherings of contactees and onlookers) were held from 1954
through 1970. Formerly an aircraft mechanic for Douglas,
Hughes, and Lockheed, George founded the Ministry of Universal Wisdom after his first 'contact'.

It was in 1951 that he was allegedly contacted for the first
time – telepathically – by the 'Council of Seven Lights'. Then
later, in 1952, he was contacted again and 'given a ride in a flying
saucer'.

As were most of the contactees, Van Tassel was very much a
technician at heart as well as by occupation. This techno-
mechanical orientation came through strongly in his technological worship of the Space People. Among his inventions (all with
the aid of secret scientific knowledge supplied by the Space
People, of course), is a structure capped with a large white
dome called the 'Integratron'. Utilising principles of 'electro-
static generation' to modify the cell structure of the human body,
Van Tassel claimed it could help to slow down the ageing process.
(Here we have, as always, the dream of immortality common to
all religions.)

It was interesting to read in a 1973 interview with Van Tassel,
in the *Desert* (Hot Springs) *Sentinel*, that he heartily recommended
von Däniken's book *Chariots of the Gods?* 'because,' he said,
'this book will inform you of ancient civilisations that accomplished fantastic things we cannot duplicate today'.[16] Obviously,
both of them have been thinking along very similar lines.

What has been written by Bryant and Helen Reeve, in their
book *Flying Saucer Pilgrimage*, expresses quite accurately, I
think, the ideas of both Van Tassel (in his alleged practice of
OSC) and von Däniken (in his book *Miracles of the Gods*):

As we understand it, the space-beings are actually directing
cosmic ideas to the earth, and these are being received inspira-
tionally by many individuals all over the world. They do not
know where these ideas come from. They are like institutions
and inspirations, but the individuals somehow feel sure that

they have received something good and fine and true. This is a characteristic of this age, and we classify this as a one-way inspirational broadcast or communication from the space-beings to their brothers and sisters on earth. It is part of the unseen help they are lovingly giving us in these critical times.[17]

Very simply put, OSC is the contactee's version of *prayer*.

Every religion also has its own special set of instructions for prudent living and proper care of the body. A contactee who emphasised such practical teachings of the Space People was Howard Menger, a sign-painter by profession and formerly a resident of High Bridge, New Jersey but now living in Vero Beach, Florida.

Menger claims the earliest of all the alleged contacts with our benevolent friends from outer space. It began in 1932, when he was only ten years old, while playing in the woods near his home. He came upon a beautiful golden-haired woman, sitting on a rock. Howard later wrote: '[she] was the most exquisite woman my young eyes had ever beheld! The warm sunlight caught the highlights of her long golden hair as it cascaded around her face and shoulders. The curves of her lovely body were delicately contoured – revealed through the translucent material of [her] clothing . . .' The woman said, 'Howard, I have come a long way to see you . . . and to talk to you.' She told him, '*We are contacting our own*'.[18] She explained that when he grew older, he would be contacted again (ie when he could understand their teachings, which would include the knowledge of his purpose on Earth and what would be expected of him as a messenger of the Space People).

Indeed, there were other meetings with the Space People, a long series of contacts which included a course of instruction that continued over many years and amounted to a complete guide to good, clean living. Spiritual subjects were taught, such as the proper care of the soul, but also there were teachings about the proper care of the body. Special health foods were extremely important. When the Space People visited Earth, but neglected to bring along their own food, 'They asked mainly for frozen fruit juices, canned fruit and vegetables, whole wheat bread, wheat germ and the like.'[19] One specimen of food processed by the Space People, a lunar potato, was given to a laboratory in Philadelphia for their analysis. It was found, according to Menger, to have five times more protein than potatoes grown on the Earth.[20]

I hope my point is now clear – namely that the imaginary Space Gods of von Däniken are little more than modern replacements for the 'Space Brothers' created by the contactees in the 1950s.

The books of von Däniken, his imitators and predecessors, although labelled by their publishers as 'non-fiction', are, nevertheless, usually classified in bookstores under the 'occult' heading. I find the honesty of those booksellers admirable in letting us know the proper category in which the Space-God theory belongs.*

SOURCE NOTES

1 Frieda Fordham, *An Introduction to Jung's Psychology* (Harmondsworth, Middlesex: Penguin Books, 1953, 1966), pp65–6.
2 Carl G. Jung, *Flying Saucers: A Modern Myth of Things Seen in the Skies*, trans. R. F. C. Hull (London: Routledge & Kegan Paul, 1959, 1977), pp19–21.
3 Ibid., pxiii.
4 Ibid., pxiv.
5 William Howells, *The Heathens*, p17.
6 Robert S. Ellwood, Jr., 'Religious Movements and UFOs', in *The Encyclopaedia of UFOs* (London: New English Library, forthcoming).
7 *Chariots of the Gods?* pp146–7.

*For two contrasting discussions of the many occult and religious aspects of 'ancient astronauts' and UFOs, see: *UFOs – God's Chariots?* by Ted Peters (Atlanta, Georgia: John Knox Press, 1977); and *Close Encounters: A Better Explanation* by Clifford Wilson and John Weldon (San Diego, California: Master Books, 1978).

137

8 Erich von Däniken, *Miracles of the Gods* (London: Corgi Books, 1977), p199.

9 Ibid., p202.

10 George Adamski, *Behind the Flying Saucer Mystery* (New York: Warner Paperback Library, 1961, 1974), p83.

11 *The Book of the Prophet Ezekiel*, commentary by Keith W. Carley (London: Cambridge University Press, 1974).

12 Adamski, p84.

13 Orfeo Angelucci, *The Secret of the Saucers* (Amherst, Wisconsin: Amherst Press, 1955), pii.

14 Ibid., pp1–13.

15 C. G. Jung, pp162 and 166.

16 *Desert* (Hot Springs, California) *Sentinel*, 23 August 1973.

17 Bryant and Helen Reeve, *Flying Saucer Pilgrimage* (Amherst, Wisconsin: Amherst Press, 1957), p195.

18 Howard Menger, *From Outer Space to You* (Clarksburg, West Virginia: Saucerian Books, 1959), pp26–7.

19 Ibid., p73.

20 Ibid., pp138–9.

In *The Space-Gods Revealed*, I expressed the opinion that UFO-cult groups that play upon the credulity (and even neuroses and psychoses) of distressed minds should not be confused with serious, qualified UFO researchers. Famed writer of science fiction and science fact, Arthur C. Clarke, was attempting to draw a similar distinction, I think, when he wrote:

A small proportion of UFOs have never been satisfactorily explained, and the theory that they are visitors from outer space is a perfectly reasonable one; I would be the last to condemn it, since I have spent most of my life expounding the possibility.

What I *am* condemning is the credulous naïveté of those who have accepted this theory and made almost a religion of it. On the strength of a few faked photographs and the ravings of obviously psychopathic personalities, thousands were convinced that men from space had actually landed on this Earth.[1]

Clarke has modified his position somewhat, however, in his recent book, *The View From Serendip* (1977), in which he expresses the opinion that the interstellar spaceship theory of UFOs '. . . can no longer be taken very seriously'.[2] Although my own view on the subject of UFOs is one of curiosity more than 'belief', I do feel that a genuine UFO mystery exists, in sharp contrast to the fraudulent, manufactured pseudo-mysteries associated with imaginary 'ancient astronauts'. That does not mean, of course, that hoaxes and phony evidence does not exist in the UFO field. God knows – it is abundant. But the same is true for almost any controversial field of study, and because UFOlogy is so inherently bizarre, it naturally attracts the fun-loving as well as the curious.

There are also numerous misidentifications and reports of 'objects' with which the observer is not familiar and hence for that person become 'UFOs'. Most of these 'mistakes' turn out to be weather balloons, aircraft, astronomical objects (stars and planets), or other natural phenomena (ball lightning, unusual clouds, etc). But what gives rise to the 'mystery' is that even after such reasonable explanations are taken into account, there still remains a residue of seemingly inexplicable phenomena; things and events which do not seem to fit reasonably into any acceptable framework of existing human knowledge (see illus 80–85). (This is assuming, of course, that much of the data can be taken at face value. And in order to be consistent with other branches of knowledge and accepted common practice – in areas such as jurisprudence, for example – we must be willing to ascribe some measure of validity to eye-witness reports.)

There is no question but that UFOlogy has become more respectable in recent years, both among scientists and the general public. There have been at least four PhD dissertations written on the subject and according to a recent (1977) survey of 1,356 professional astromoners, 53% of the respondents believe that UFOs 'certainly' or 'probably' should be investigated further. In France, the National Centre for Space Studies (CNES, roughly the French equivalent of NASA in the United States) has created an official government research group, under the directorship of astronomer Claude Poher, to study the UFO phenomenon.

Public opinion polls in the United States have revealed a striking increase in pro-UFO sentiment over the last twenty-five years. In the early 1950s, when 'flying saucers' first became a sensational topic for newspapers and popular magazines around the world, only 11% of the US population were 'believers'. By 1957, this figure more than doubled to 25%, then rose to 46% in

1966, 51 % in 1973, and now according to the latest (1978) Gallup Poll, 57 % of Americans who have heard or read about UFOs believe they represent a real phenomenon.

For the past 26 years, the Aerial Phenomena Research Organisation (APRO) has served as the focal point of first-hand UFO reports from all over the world. In fact, the majority of most of the 'classic' UFO cases that have been publicised in books, periodicals, and movies over the past quarter of a century came from APRO's files. In February 1976, I tape-recorded the following brief interview with the founders of APRO, James (Jim) and Coral Lorenzen (who reside in Tucson, Arizona, as does the author):

RS: I think it would be interesting to hear from both of you what the early years of the UFO controversy were like. When things first started to happen, what did people think?

CL: For me, it started happening in 1934, when I was nine; I saw something. I was called 'crazy', and because I wore glasses, some of the other kids said, 'Well, she can't see,' and so on. So, when 1947 came along, and all the sightings started, it was just a matter of: well, I wasn't so crazy after all. And by then, I had read Charles Fort's books, and I started saving clippings, like a lot of people, and in the fall of 1951 – Jim and I were both very interested in it – I told Jim: 'You know, someone ought to be collecting this stuff, because it's being printed and that's it. It goes into newspaper files, it's burned up, or whatever.' So, in January '52, I started APRO.

JL: The kind of mood that I remember about 1947, '48, '49, and '50, was that there was quite a bit of anecdotal material that appeared in magazines and in the press [newspapers] and there was always a kind of expectation that, well, pretty soon we'll know what it is.

RS: Everybody expected that the answer was going to be delivered at any moment, and no one really questioned the sightings? In other words, the general attitude was: there is a mystery, but we think it's going to be solved very soon.

JL: Well, there were some people who volunteered the opinion

141

that there was nothing to this, and the mystery was 'solved' many times.

CL: Immediately, the categories came out: Russian missiles, American secret weapons, hallucinations, and that was the beginning. Then, after Menzel [Professor Donald Menzel of Harvard University] got into it, in 1952, this conception of mundane objects and so forth – planets and stars—

JL: —spider webs—

RS: Yes, what struck me about Menzel was how he seemed to get so overly *emotional* when he argued the negative side of the controversy.

CL: Well, let me tell you – the people who made a pronouncement early in the game, and then saw, progressively through the years, that people were not only seeing things going through the sky; the things started to land. There were reports of landings, reports of occupants. Menzel was in the category of the people who had shot off his mouth too quickly; he judged too soon.

JL: Yes, I think the way he got into this was that *Look* magazine wanted to interview Willy Ley, who was a well-known expert on outer space subjects. They wanted to interview him and have him talk about UFOs, but he didn't want to, and he recommended that *Look* interview, instead, Dr Donald Menzel who was both a science-fiction writer and a professor of astronomy. Willy Ley said that Menzel had some theories about this, and he had set up a little experiment where he showed that temperature inversions could produce reflections. But the fact of the matter is that you only get optical reflections off an inversion layer at angles of about four degrees. So, if you see anything at elevations of greater than four degrees, it's probably not a reflection off an inversion layer.

RS: Yes, one thing that bothered me too – when he talked about the Washington National sightings, he said they were temperature inversions. Why haven't they appeared that way before and—

CL: —haven't since?

RS: Right.

JL: And the inversion wasn't that well pronounced that night either, according to the Weather Bureau. And McDonald [the late Dr James E. McDonald, atmospheric physicist of the University of Arizona] pointed out that an atmospheric inversion is only about as reflective as a pane of window glass, which again would not account for the bright objects observed over Washington [DC] that night.

RS: It would seem to me that more people should have seen inversions as an obvious phenomenon if it really was something that could produce an illusion so striking that jets would take to the air and so on.

CL: Have you ever seen a 'sun dog'?

RS: Yes.

CL: And to see a sun dog, and say that that is what people are identifying as flying saucers is ridiculous.

JL: I have seen automobile headlights reflected off an inversion layer, but all it looks like is this: for a brief moment, you will see two sets of headlights and then they will disappear. Just for that brief moment when you are looking along that angle of about four degrees. It is a very short-lived phenomenon.

RS: I think that is another weakness in some of the UFO 'explanations' – the fact that the natural phenomenon that is supposed to explain the UFO is oftentimes a phenomenon of short duration, and not the sort of thing that stays in view for twenty minutes while a jet chases after it.

JL: There was a case out at Red Bluff, California involving some Sheriff's Deputies, quite a few years back. Menzel explained it as temperature inversions, but these guys were talking about elevations of fifteen and twenty degrees, and Menzel said they were inversions of some planets and stars that had not yet risen.

RS: But then, I've also heard of cases such as the one that took place here in Tucson, in which a whole caravan of cars went off chasing the planet Venus.

JL: Yes, they do. Some people have been fooled by stars and planets, but such cases are relatively rare.

RS: One thing that bothers me is that UFO cases are seemingly never tracked down all the way and investigated to the hilt, to the point of a definitive analysis, leaving no stones unturned.

JL: No one really has the budget to do it. We get to where we are fairly sure of how it would be if we went all the way.

RS: Not even the Air Force did it. In his book, *The Report on Unidentified Flying Objects* (Doubleday, 1956), Ruppelt talked as if, at one point, they had all the resources they needed to check out these things. Yet there were still no really *thorough* investigations, at least to my knowledge. The conclusions were always left hanging.

JL: Well, on paper it said they did, but when you get down to actually doing it, then there was always a problem. In other words, theoretically, you have all the resources of the entire Air Force at your disposal, but when it comes to requisitioning some service, then the guy says, 'I don't know anything about that. No I can't OK that.' You have to buck it up to a higher level. You get bound up in red tape. And if you need somebody's lab, you really don't get to use it when you need it, because of paperwork.

RS: I read somewhere the criticism that instead of the Air Force statement that was usually given to the effect that a given case could not be solved because of 'insufficient information', they should have said 'insufficient follow up'.

JL: Yes. You see my idea is that Project Blue Book, after Ruppelt, didn't follow anything up because that really wasn't their job. Their assignment was to explain it away.

RS: A public relations function?

JL: Yes. And Air Force regulation 200-2 advises the commanding officer turning the investigation over to the AISS [Air Intelligence Services Squadron], and the AISS was a kind of secret outfit with a few men at each base. And I think that has been changed now, but at the time, that's what it was. So if it was a good case, it never got to Blue Book.

RS: This is one of the key questions, for me: is there some kind of investigation going on at a higher level than what the American public has been told about?

JL: Well, there *has* to be. The normal kind of investigation that is carried out every time there is something unexplained occurring in the Zone of the Interior (ZI).

RS: In other words, you are saying that it is unthinkable that some-body connected with the United States government is not still carrying on some kind of investigation of UFOs – and it would more than likely be the CIA?

JL: Yeah, sure, because if you've got an unidentified vehicle in our air space, it can't be ignored. You can't ignore it. There are all kinds of possibilities: a Russian spy plane, or a missile, or a bomber; you really can't ignore it.

RS: And yet, if there really is a good surveillance system in opera-tion, how is it that, if they [the US government] really want to debunk a given UFO, they can't just simply say: 'Well, this particular object happens to be a such and such'; and it would seem that it would be a simple matter to prove just exactly what each and every UFO really is.

CS: They can't do that because you've got people at a lower level who know what's going on there. There are people at a local level who know what was or was not there at the time, and there's the danger of a leak.

RS: What about the stories of the mysterious 'men in black', or other suspicious characters, who have been said to have ap-proached various UFO witnesses with warnings that the witness keep silent about his experience or else suffer some sinister consequence?

CL: We've got this Travis Walton case, at Snowflake. It's a beauty. He's passed the lie detector and the whole bit. Neither he, nor his brother, nor any of the witnesses, nor we, have been ap-proached by any kind of governmental agency. But, I figure that if the government has got a study going, all they have to do is subscribe to our bulletin and the various other ones, monitor the situation, and we're going to do their work for them anyway. We have been for twenty-five years.

RS: Just briefly, what is your theory of the origin and nature of the UFOs?

JL: Well, if you stand back a little and just look at the evidence – I mean let the evidence lead you – the pattern you get is that of a number of alien types working in concert to get an idea of what's going on on this planet, including a complete psycho-logical profile of the human race.

145

The Lorenzens' theory, which is shared by many of APRO's scientific consultants, is one intriguing possibility. But, as always, to be prudent, we should keep aware of human psychological factors which may influence our perceptions, our beliefs, and may cloud our judgment – especially with regard to such provocative ideas.

Historically, the first major wave of UFO sightings (in 1947) came at a crucial period for the world in general, and for the United States in particular. We were in the midst of the so-called 'Cold War'; when diplomatic relations between the US and the USSR were so strained and uncertain that neither side felt totally safe from a surprise attack. By the early 1950s a great deal of effort was directed towards the development of long-range ballistic missiles capable of carrying nuclear warheads. Never had there been a time in history when more attention was given to observing the sky, and with so much fearful apprehension.

There is little wonder, under these circumstances, that one of the first theories seriously considered by the Air Technical Intelligence Center (ATIC) of the US Air Force to explain the sudden phenomenon of 'flying saucer' reports, in the late 40s and early 50s, was that the Russians might be testing a new secret weapon. Both the Americans and the Russians had, at the end of World War II, captured their share of top German scientists who, during the war, had been developing rocket designs far superior to the known capabilities of any of the other world powers.

Captain Edward J. Ruppelt, former chief of Project Blue Book (formerly, the official UFO unit of the US Air Force), offered the following comments in his book, *The Report on Unidentified Flying Objects* (1956):

When World War II ended, the Germans had several radical types of aircraft and guided missiles under development. The majority of these projects were in the most preliminary stages but they were the only craft that could even approach the performance of the objects reported by UFO observers. Like the Allies, after World War II, the Soviets had obtained complete sets of data on the latest German developments. This,

146

coupled with rumours that the Soviets were frantically developing the German ideas, caused no small degree of alarm. As more UFOs were observed near the Air Force's Muroc Test Center, the Army's White Sands Proving Ground, and atomic bomb plants, ATIC's efforts became more concentrated. Wires were sent to intelligence agents in Germany requesting that they find out exactly how much progress had been made on the various German projects. The last possibility, of course, was that the Soviets had discovered some completely new aerodynamic concept that would give saucer performance.[3]

One of the first professional journalists to cover the story of the mysterious flying discs was retired Marine Major Donald E. Keyhoe. Keyhoe also considered the possibility of a new secret weapon that might be under development by either the Soviet Union, Great Britain, or the United States. What gave some credence to the idea, for Keyhoe, was the curtain of official secrecy that he encountered while pursuing his own investigations. Working at first for editor Ken Purdy of *True* magazine, Keyhoe travelled the country interviewing pilots, engineers, Air Force public relations officers, and anyone who might offer a lead that could later prove helpful. When even his old friends in the military could not (or would not, he thought) reveal all they knew about the mystery of the 'saucers', he sensed a high-level cover-up. The idea of a secret military device seemed plausible, at first, but there was one serious drawback to the theory. It just didn't make sense that a new secret missile would be tested openly, over populated areas, risking the possibility of a crash-landing and recovery by the wrong persons. It would just be far too easy for the secret to fall into the wrong hands. Once Keyhoe finally rejected the secret missile theory, he found himself, reluctantly, so he says, opting in favour of the interplanetary theory to account for the origin of the flying discs. In his first book, *The Flying Saucers Are Real* (1950), Keyhoe states his conclusions under three main points:

1 The Earth has been under periodic observation from another planet, or other planets, for at least two centuries.
2 This observation suddenly increased in 1947, following the

series of A-bomb explosions begun in 1945.

3 The observation, now intermittent, is part of a long-range survey and will continue indefinitely. No immediate attempt to contact the Earth seems evident. There may be some unknown block to making contact, but it is more probable that the spacemen's plans are not complete.[4]

There are, no doubt, sufficient psychological reasons alone to account for the popularity of the interplanetary spaceship theory, but there are a few rational considerations as well. Some of the main points that have been made in favour of the spaceship theory are these:

(1) There have been many thousands of observations of strange lights and shapes seen in the sky which *seemingly* exhibit volition and intentional manoeuvring, making them appear to be under some kind of intelligent control.

(2) The known technology of Earth does not seem to be as far advanced as that of the 'objects' observed.*

(3) It seems unthinkable, in the light of recent theories about the origin of life on our own planet, considered together with the vastness of the known universe, that the Earth is the only planet on which intelligent life has developed.

One possibility that we should not, perhaps, dismiss too lightly is that of a monitoring system that might have been set up to keep track of our progress, of which the UFOs may be a part. Computer scientist Jacques Vallée, formerly of Stanford University, has suggested that UFOs may even be part of a 'control system' intended to influence our thoughts and behaviour. The following extract, taken from Dr Vallée's book, *The Invisible College* (1975), will help explain his theory:

*ie *if* it is indeed *technology* that we are observing.

I propose the hypothesis that there is a control system for human consciousness. I have not been able to determine whether it is natural or spontaneous; whether it is explainable in terms of genetics, of social psychology, or of ordinary phenomena – or if it is artificial in nature, and under the power of some superhuman will. It may be entirely determined by laws that we have not yet discovered . . .

[I am suggesting] . . . that what takes place through close encounters with UFOs is control of human beliefs, control of the relationship between our consciousness and physical reality, that this control has been in force throughout history, and that it is of secondary importance that it should now assume the form of sightings of space visitors.

When the object we call UFO is visible to us in the reality of everyday life, I think that it constitutes *both* a physical entity with mass, inertia, volume, etc, which we can measure, *and* a window towards another mode of reality for at least some of the participants. Is this why witnesses can give us at the same time a consistent narrative . . . and a description of contact with forms of life that fit no acceptable framework? These forms of life may be similar to projections; they may be real, yet a product of our dreams. Like our dreams, they may also shape what we think of as our lives in ways that we do not yet understand.[5]

Another leading Ufologist, Dr J. Allen Hynek, formerly Chairman of the Astronomy Department at Northwestern University, Evanston, Illinois, and former astronomical consultant to the US Air Force Projects Sign and Blue Book for more than twenty years, has expressed his position on the UFO problem this way:

I am . . . inclined to think in terms of something meta-terrestrial – a sort of parallel reality . . .

I have the impression that the UFOs are announcing a change that is coming soon in our scientific paradigms. I am very much afraid that UFOs are related to certain psychic phenomena. And if I say 'I am very much afraid', this is

149

because in our Center [CUFOS, the Center for UFO Studies] at Evanston we are trying to study this problem from the angle of the physical sciences . . . But it would be absurd to follow up only one path to the exclusion of all the others.[6]

Certainly the phenomenon has psychic aspects. I don't talk about them very much because to a general audience the words 'psychic' and 'occult' have bad overtones. They say, 'Aw, it's all crazy.' But the fact is that there are psychic things; for instance, UFOs seem to materialise and dematerialise. There are people who've had UFO experiences who've claimed to have developed psychic ability. There have been reported cases of healings in close encounters and there have been reported cases of precognition, where people had foreknowledge or forewarning that they were going to see something. There has been a change of outlook, a change of philosophy of persons' lives. Now you see, those are rather tricky things to talk about openly, but it's there.

Many people, like Jacques Vallée and I, to some extent, feel that it might be a conditioning process.[7]

Whether or not such phenomena are being controlled by a non-human intelligence or whether they are merely the 'psychic concomitants' of a 'visionary rumour', as Carl Jung implied, we do not know. But it can be said, with certainty, that a psychological 'conditioning process' *is* taking place, which is either directly or indirectly related to the UFO phenomenon.

When confronted with this, I cannot help but draw the immediate conclusion that even if we must wait for the ultimate answer (which I feel will come, some day) to the physical and/or metaphysical aspects of the UFO question, we can, in the meanwhile, learn something about *ourselves*.

The UFO controversy is a microcosm of the universe of ideas that forms our basic concepts of science, religion, politics, and law. Extraterrestrial speculation touches virtually every subject area that man tends to think deeply about. The very idea of Space-Gods and UFOs (the perennial 'omens in the sky') capable of influencing or even *controlling* human society is much more even than an age-old archetype of the human psyche; it serves as the most perfect common denominator of all time, allowing modern interpretations for old-time religion. All the more reason to recognise the great 'cosmic looking-glass', that can reveal our own true natures. As Alvin Toffler once put it: 'What we think, imagine or dream about cultures beyond Earth not only reflects our own hidden fears and wishes, but alters them.'[8]

Looking deeply into the complex problem of UFOs and possible extraterrestrial intelligence forces us to operate at a 'meta-level' of philosophical thought that may just serve to sharpen our use of logic and true scientific method even if we do not, at first, find all the answers we are looking for. Perhaps our studies will reveal the true nature of our objectivity – or lack of it. The very concepts of 'evidence' and 'proof' are pushed to the limit, taking us ultimately into the realm of the philosophy of science.

In the end, we should be more able to fulfil the dictum of Socrates: 'Know thyself.'

SOURCE NOTES
1 Arthur C. Clarke, *Voices From the Sky* (New York: Pyramid Books, 1967), p169.
2 Arthur C. Clarke, *The View From Serendip* (New York: Ballantine Books, 1977), p161.
3 Edward J. Ruppelt, *The Report on Unidentified Flying Objects* (Garden City, New York: Doubleday & Co., 1956), pp39–40.
4 Donald Keyhoe, *The Flying Saucers Are Real* (New York: Fawcett Publications, 1950), p174.
5 Jacques Vallée, *The Invisible College* (New York: E. P. Dutton, 1976), p196.
6 Interview in *Lumières dans la Nuit*, No 168, October 1977.
7 Interview in *Today's Student*, 3 April 1978.
8 Magoroh Maruyama and Arthur Harkins, eds., *Cultures Beyond the Earth* (New York: Vintage Books/Random House, 1975), Foreword, pvii.

TIPTOEING BEYOND DARWIN:
AN EXAMINATION OF SOME UNCONVENTIONAL
THEORIES ON THE ORIGIN OF MAN
by
J. Richard Greenwell

The concept of the ancient astronauts, the idea that extraterrestrials visited Earth in times past and transmitted new knowledge to early civilisations, has captured the public imagination, and has been promoted by numerous writers. A close examination of these claims has found no evidence that such visitations ever occurred (Story 1976, 1977).

The purpose of this treatise is to address critically some related claims: that man, rather than having evolved through a process of natural selection and other evolutionary forces, is a result of 1) cross-breeding between extraterrestrials and ape-men, or the genetic manipulation of ape-men (the hybrid hypothesis), or 2) an extraterrestrial transplant to Earth, and that he is not even related to the primates (the transplant hypothesis). The original extraterrestrials, many believe, have since maintained a parental eye over mankind, thus the many UFO reports since the practical application of nuclear energy.

The best known of the hybrid hypothesis proponents are probably Brinsley Le Poer Trench (1960, 1969, 1973), and Erich von Däniken (1969, 1970, 1973, 1977). However, the most lucid argument supporting the hypothesis is a book by Max Flindt and Otto Binder (1974), based on a smaller manuscript published privately by Flindt in 1962, entitled *On Tiptoe Beyond Darwin*. They postulate that 'whenever hominid species in the past made inexplicable leaps ahead, in any area, those leaps had one common cause – *the biomanipulations of the starmen.*'

Specifically, they claim: 1) that man's primate ancestors were brought down from the trees to become bipedal by the artificial introduction of dominant genes for upright walking; 2) that *Ramapithecus* was genetically 'improved' 12 million years ago, thus explaining the lack of intermediate fossils between it and *Australopithecus*; 3) that *Homo erectus* was physically transported to those areas where his remains have been found, being unable to migrate to those locations because of the 'fierce predators' of the time; 4) that the demise of *Homo erectus* was planned in order to allow Neanderthal, the new, improved man, to survive; 5) that something went 'wrong' with Neanderthal after a 75,000 year trial-period; and 6) that Cro-Magnon (modern) man was finally the 'successful' bioengineering feat of the extraterrestrials.

Flindt and Binder have accumulated an enormous but selective amount of evolutionary, paleontogical, anatomical, physiological, neurological, and behavioural data, and seem truly puzzled by 'gaps' and 'mysteries', which they solve with the sweeping, all encompassing explanation of extraterrestrial intervention. The fact is that most of the 'mysteries' are not nearly as mysterious as they believe, or are not mysteries at all if one has even a rudimentary understanding of the close relationship between changing environments and evolution, and the resulting integrated functions of the senses, morphology, and behaviour.

For example, they state: 'If the forests did not decline but grew more lushly as time passed, why in the world should a tree-dwelling species of animal desert his original habitat? It is questions like these that tongue-tie the anthropologists.' In fact, our ancestors probably came down from the trees and consequently became bipedal not because they *wanted* to, but because they *had* to. Climatic changes in Miocene East Africa created isolated pockets of desiccation; the resulting deforestation, plus pressure from monkey radiation, undoubtedly increased competition among hominoid species. The strong ones, ancestors of today's great apes, claimed the remaining trees: the weaker ones, our ancestors, were forced onto the marginal lands or the arid savannahs, where they became bipedal by necessity (Hockett and Ascher 1964). It is even possible that man's biological and social development have, in part, been a result of adaption to arid zones (Greenwell 1978).

Von Däniken, another hybrid hypothesis proponent, claims that, 'If the climate drove the apes down from the trees during the following millenia, that must have included all kinds of apes and not just the one which selected to prodice *homo* [sic]*sapiens*' (1973). Von Däniken sees this as proof of outside intervention: if descending from the trees led to tool-making and intelligence, 'there should not really be any apes left today'. These statements ignore the very important factor of ecological dominance. The stronger apes *stayed* in the trees, and *remained* as apes.

Flindt and Binder pass over the question of *Homo erectus*' intelligence, which was far superior to that of the 'fierce predators' to be encountered in migrations; even the beginnings of language (and the resulting social cooperation) can far outweigh any animal's advantages in speed, bulk, or offensive characteristics. They also seem to subscribe to the Victorian image of Neanderthal as a dumb and clumsy brute, something that went 'wrong'. Neanderthal is now seen in a new light, and is accorded (at least in American anthropology) the status of the first true man, probably with language and a concept of death, and maybe life after death (Leroi-Gourhan 1975, Solecki 1975).

They also ask why man alone became intelligent, why his brain weight is relatively higher than that of other animals, why some Neanderthals had larger braincases than modern man, why man alone can 'speak words', why man alone can make tools, and why human civilisation sprang up 'abruptly'. All of these kinds of questions have simple and/or conventional answers. One example is man's almost unique hairlessness, which they attribute to his descent from hairless extraterrestrials. An alternate hypothesis is that a reduction in body hair came about through an increased sweating need in strenuous, open-country hunting (Montagu 1964). Other hypotheses have been reviewed by Cloudsley-Thompson (1975).

In an attempt to 'prove' the hybrid hypothesis, Flindt and Binder point out the anatomical and physiological distance that separates man from the apes, and quote from Sir Arthur Keith, a distinguished British physical anthropologist from early in the century, who listed the number of individual, generic characteristics of man, apes, and monkeys, based on many years of anatomical study (Keith 1911). They believe that Keith's data elevate their own case to a plateau so high that it challenges the Darwinian theory of evolution. This question will be addressed in more detail below.

Von Däniken even goes a step beyond the hybrid hypothesis. He believes that man's extraterrestrial ancestors were the losers in a cataclysmic cosmic battle (1973). Like Flindt and Binder, von Däniken is mystified by human evolution, and raises questions which, to him, can only be answered in terms of extraterrestrial, genetic intervention (1969, 1970, 1977). A careful review of the questions he raises, however, finds them all perfectly soluble within the framework of conventional theory in human evolution.

The other major school of thought believes that man was 'transplanted' here, and is not even genetically related to the primates. Richard Mooney (1974, 1975), for example, dismisses the idea of cross-breeding or genetic manipulation, claiming that 'there is only a superficial physical resemblance between the anthropoid apes and man' (1974). He states, curiously, that his theory 'solves the problems of man on Earth without invoking either evolution or miraculous creation'.

Although he presents less data than Flindt and Binder, Mooney goes so far as to propose that man was placed on Earth as recently as 40,000 years ago ('with clothes, fire, weapons, shelter and with a native ability and intelligence that is certainly no less that that possessed by peoples of the present time'), and interprets paleoanthropological data in such a way so as to support this astonishing proposition. Mooney questions why hominids appeared only in the last million years, and not in the Miocene and Pliocene, 'an ideal time for the presursors of humanity to have appeared'. Our hominid precursors, in fact, *did* appear in the Miocene or Pliocene, but Mooney has confused the human lineage of hominids, which evolved about 10–15 million years ago, with the human genus *Homo*, which evolved about five million years ago.

A number of specific characteristics shared mutually by man and the primates, particularly the great apes, will now be examined. Entire volumes could be, and have been, written on such morphological and physiological similarities, so we shall

156

restrict ourselves to a few important ones. These will clearly demonstrate the intimate evolutionary linkages man has with his primate relatives.

Before we proceed, two points are in order. First, it should be noted that primates, as an order, are very 'generalised'. That is they have few morphological features adapted for highly specialised functions. This has permitted their successful adaptation to a wide range of environments. Thus, we find today that some species are strictly arboreal, while others are only terrestrial; some are nocturnal, others diurnal; some inhabit humid, tropical rain forests, others dry grasslands or even deserts; some eat only vegetable matter, others only fruits, or insects, and so forth. These wide adaptive differences have even led to disagreements concerning whether or not some species should be included in the order. It is therefore not at all surprising that the hybrid hypothesis proponents, unversed as they are in primatology, should interpret the many differences that do exist between man and ape as something mysterious.

The second point to be made is that morphological and physiological evidence, plus the evidence of fossils, tell us that today's prosimians, New World monkeys, Old World monkeys, apes, and man, represent, in ascending order, specific branches or stages of primate evolution over the past 60 or so million years. Clearly, today's prosimians, for example, are not exactly what they were, say, 40 million years ago, but they *do* represent the morphological and physiological characteristics the prosimians had at that time, or even earlier. We thus have, today, a living laboratory of primate evolution. As we shall now see, this living laboratory provides the data needed to verify man's direct descent from primate ancestors, without having to resort to genetic manipulation by extraterrestrials, or other such ideas.

The Evidence of Genetic Biology: Amino acid sequencing of homologous proteins, and immunological and electrophoretic methods of protein comparisons have demonstrated that human polypeptides (chains of amino acids which form protein molecules) are more than 99 % identical to those of the chimpanzee (King and Wilson 1975). The genetic distance

157

between humans and chimpanzees is so small, in fact, that it corresponds to that between sibling (closely allied) species, and is less than between two non-sibling species of the same genus. As man and chimpanzee do not even belong to the same family, these findings indicate that structural gene evolution and morphological evolution may proceed at different rates, a proposition further supported by a comparative study of the morphological differences between man and chimpanzee and two dissimilar species of frogs (Cherry, Case, and Wilson 1978). At the same time, it also demonstrates the very real genetic closeness between man and chimpanzee.

This genetic closeness is again confirmed by the similarity between the 46 chromosomes of man and the 48 chromosomes of the great apes (Chiarelli 1972, Miller 1977). General and regional bonding methods of human and primate chromosomes have established that the karyotypes (arranged microphotographs of chromosomes) of man, chimpanzee, and gorilla are very similar, so much so that it is difficult to establish their evolutionary distinction (Miller 1977). These studies also indicate that the gorilla may actually be evolutionarily closer to man than the chimpanzee.

The blood proteins of primates have also been analysed and compared (Goodman, Koen, Barnabas, and Moore 1972, Wilson and Sarich 1969). Predictably, the serum proteins of tree shrews (the most 'primitive' of the primates) and other prosimians are the least like those of man, but they are nevertheless more like man's than those of all other non-primate mammals. The New World monkeys come next, followed by the Old World monkeys, and two of the apes, the gorilla and the chimpanzee. The serum proteins of the orangutan and, in particular, the gibbon differ more markedly. The comparison of polypeptides, chromosomes, and blood proteins demonstrate a definite evolutionary linkage between man and all the primates, particularly the apes.

The Evidence of the Digestive System: The alimentary tract of all primates is quite similar (with the exception of the African leaf-eating monkey species, which have relatively large and sacculated stomachs, necessitated by their diet). Even the tree shrew's digestive system is quite similar to that of man (Clark 1963). While the liver of monkey species is located in a different position from that of the apes and man, the latter two have the liver attached in the same place, underneath the diaphragm. It can be stated that 'the four (modern) anthropoid apes and man possess in common a number of visceral characters that clearly pronounce their affinities' (Strauss 1936).

The Evidence of Parasites: The great apes and man are hosts to more of the same parasites than man shares with any other mammals (Dunn 1966). Again predictably, man shares most of these (over 50 % in one parasite genera) with the chimpanzee and the gorilla, fewer with the orangutan, and even less with the gibbon. It is also apparent that the malarial parasites of man and every one of the apes evolved from a common ancestor. This is an important point, as it indicates that their hosts, man and apes, did likewise.

The Evidence of Dentition: Human dentition varies from ape dentition in several important features: the dental 'arch' is curved in man, while in the apes it is squared. Human canines are small and blunt, and erupt early in life, while in the apes they are large, pointed, and erupt later in life. There are other differences too, but the overall dentition pattern of both is strikingly similar, implying a common origin. The differences can certainly be explained by ecological and adaptive factors.

One of the most important similarities between man and apes is in the dental formula. With the exception of the marmosets, the dental formula for the more 'primitive' New World monkeys (and also for some of the lemurs) is $\frac{2 \cdot 1 \cdot 3 \cdot 3 \cdot}{2 \cdot 1 \cdot 3 \cdot 3}$. That is, each side of the upper jaw and lower jaw has two incisors, one canine, three premolars, and three molars. In the Old World monkeys, the dental formula is $\frac{2 \cdot 1 \cdot 2 \cdot 3 \cdot}{2 \cdot 1 \cdot 2 \cdot 3}$, and it is no coincidence that this is the same formula for both the apes and man.

The Evidence of Vision: Most primates, including man, have

159

two kinds of cellular photoreceptors, rods and cones, in their visual apparatus. The former permit vision in dim light, and the latter permit bright-light colour vision. Visibility curves, which plot sensitivity as a function of wavelength, give different maximum sensitivities in the scotopic (rod) visibility curve and the photopic (cone) visibility curve. Although visibility curves have not been determined for the apes, maximum scotopic and photopic sensitivities have been found to be very similar in both New and Old World monkeys, apes (except in scotopic curves, for which they have not been tested) and man, at 510 and 550 nanometres respectively (King and Fobes 1974). Visibility curves, according to data provided by living primates, have remained fairly constant throughout the later stages of primate evolution.

Colour vision is exceptionally good in the primates, unlike most other mammals. It has been proposed that the first fruit-bearing trees, which appeared about the same time as the first primates, may have been a contributing factor (Polyak 1957). Tests have shown that New World monkeys are protonomolous trichromats, but that the deficit is less severe in the more 'advanced' species of that suborder. Old World monkeys, chimpanzees, and, again predictably, man are normal trichromats, indicating that there has been little recent evolutionary change (King and Fobes 1974).

Stereoscopy (binocular vision) and detail accuity are two other primate features which have evolved primarily as a result of arboreal habitat. As expected, man has excellent stereoscopy and detail accuity. It can be reasonably concluded that man's visibility curves, colour vision, stereoscopy, and detail accuity all suggest his close relation to the primates.

The Evidence of Olfaction: When some mammalian insectivores took to the trees and evolved into the primate order, the need for olfactory sensitivity decreased as the need for visual sensitivity increased. We find, in fact, that the relative volume of the olfactory areas of the brain decreases through the higher primates, and, as shown below, is lowest in man (Fobes and King 1977):

non-primate insectivores	.1062 % of brain volume
tree shrews (prosimians)	.0393
lemurs (prosimians)	.0190
tarsiers (prosimians)	.0053
New World monkeys	.0016
Old World monkeys	.0011
great apes	.0007
man	.0001

This indicates a close evolutionary linkage between man and other primates, particularly the apes.

The Evidence of Audition: Auditory ability probably changed during primate evolution, as represented by the following data on the maximum hearing frequencies of several present-day mammals, including five primates:

dolphins	100,000 cycles p.s.
cats	70,000
lemurs (prosimians)	75,000
New World monkeys	46,000
Old World monkeys	45,000
chimpanzees	26,500
man	20,500

It should be noted that, while 20,000 cycles per second is about the maximum frequency at which man can hear, his best sensitivity is at about 3,000 cycles per second. The best sensitivity for the apes is about 2,000 cycles per second. The apes and man jointly share a reduced audial frequency detection capability, relatively unique among both the primates and the mammals (Fobes and King 1977).

The Evidence of the Grasp Response: All primate infants, including human babies, possess an involuntary grasp response (it can be tested by lifting the subject off the ground while it clings to a rod, or to one's fingers). This response presumably evolved as a result of the need to cling to the parent's hair in an arboreal habitat (voluntary grasp responses occur as the infant matures). Rhesus (Old World) monkeys can so grasp for over 30 minutes. Chimpanzee infants are able to grasp for up to five minutes, and human infants for up to two minutes. This indicates a definite primate feature in man, which has decreased since he adapted to terrestrial locomotion.

The Evidence of Reproductive Biology: Most mammals have placentae, which bind the developing foetus to the female uterine wall during gestation. The haemochorial placentae of the primates varyin structure, the monkeys and apes having the most elaborate. It has also been found that Old World monkeys have more structurally efficient placentae than New World monkeys (Hill 1932). Furthermore, the placentae of both the apes and man are very similar to the Old World monkeys, and all species tend to have single births, an indication, again, of an evolutionary linkage.

Concerning the reproductive organs, both male and female genitals vary from species to species, and offer little evidence of evolutionary linkages. However, while human females do not visibly exhibit monthly sexual cycles, they do experience monthly menstrual bleeding, as do Old World monkey and ape females.

The Evidence of Neotony: Neotony is a feature in which a species retains immature characteristics in the adult form, and this is particularly so in man. For example, adult humans, which have the slowest growth rate of all the primates, resemble infant chimpanzees more than they resemble adult chimpanzees. The infant chimpanzee has a human-like 'flat' face when compared to the protruding face of its parents, does not have the brow-ridge of adult chimpanzees (or early man), and has its foramen magnum (the 'socket' at the base of the skull into which the spine fits) located directly beneath the skull; as the infant matures, the foramen magnum will gradually move towards the rear of the skull in order to balance the quadrupedal adult form (von Koenigswald 1962). In man, of course, it remains at the base of the skull.

Neotony can be closely associated with the evolution of intelligence, as infancy, childhood, adulthood, and the life span itself have become increasingly longer in the apes, and even longer in man (Napier 1970). This has permitted the better acquisition of knowledge and its subsequent transmission to a new generation. At the same time, it indicates an evolutionary continuity between man and the apes. Not that man descended from today's apes, but that both descended from the same genetic stock millions of years ago.

The Evidence of the Brain: Primates are particularly distinguishable from other mammals by an increase in the size of the occipital lobe (rear part of the brain) and a remarkable progression in the size of the frontal lobe, which reaches its maximum with the great apes and man. Although primates have undergone a brain weight increase in evolution, the higher intelligence exhibited by the apes is probably more related to cerebral convolutions, which permit more efficient use of cranial space. Man's convolutional pattern is similar to that of the apes, but is even more complex; his relative brain weight is more than double, and his absolute brain size, some 1,400 cubic centimetres, is about three times that of the apes.

Nevertheless, the increased cortical representation for vision versus the decreased olfactory representation, the increase in the frontal lobe size, and, above all, the increase in the complexity of the cerebral covolutions, which reach a high degree in the apes in general and man in particular, indicate an evolutionary linkage which is not only beyond dispute, but unique in the Earth's natural history.

The Evidence of Intelligence: While 'intelligence' can be a controversial word when used among certain behavioural scientists, it can be stated, nevertheless, that the apes are the most 'intelligent' of the non-human primates. This has been confirmed in many specially devised tests. Furthermore, numerous chimpanzees trained in computer console use, plastic symbol representation, and American Sign Language use, have shown extraordinary abilities in the expression of true language, one of the last bastions reserved for man. Language displacement (the mental manipulation of objects or events in time and space) and reconstitution (the joining

163

together of two separately learnt symbols to form a unit, ie 'waterbird' for duck) have been amply demonstrated.

The great apes undoubtedly exhibit the most advanced intelligence known to man, except for man himself. This can only be a further confirmation of the evolutionary linkages between the two.

Having reviewed some important features shared by man and the non-human primates, particularly the great apes, it can reasonably be concluded that all descended from common progenitors. No evidence has so far been presented supporting the hypothesis of man's partial or total extraterrestrial origin which survives critical scrutiny.

It is the opinion of Flindt and Binder (1974) that scientists should subject their hybrid hypothesis data to computer analysis. They do ' . . . *not* feel it necessary to bow to the verdict of scientists and their opinions . . . computers do not become swayed by such human failures.' They do, however, offer to bow to a computer verdict. Despite this, such an enterprise would serve little purpose. Computers cannot make the kind of definitive judgments Flindt and Binder seem to expect of them, and the data they would submit for analysis would be too selective and biased. A computer analysis can only be as valid as the data used.

They claim, for example, that Sir Arthur Keith's data on the number of individual characteristics of man and ape proves their case. Specifically, they state that Keith's data:

is of *paramount importance* as scientific support for the Hybrid Man theory. Out of it leaps the tremendous fact: Of the higher primates, Man has 312 physiological characteristics *peculiar to humans alone*, many more than any other species. Does this sound as though Man were some 'close relation' to the great apes? Not if Man has *three times as many differences* from his 'fellow primates' as any of the other specimens. This seems to us convincing evidence that significantly lifts our concept out of the hypothetical class into a bona-fide theory. And into a theory with such immense supportive evidence that it can, in our opinion, seriously challenge the classic Theory of Evolution.

This is a very serious statement, and the basis for such a revolutionary new theory certainly deserves further examination. First, it should be emphasised that what is important is not the number of individual characteristics man possesses *separate* from the apes, but, rather, the number of characteristics he shares *with* the apes. The sharing of such characteristics, from lower primate to higher primate, and finally to man, is the only true indicator of evolutionary linkages (or the lack of them, if such shared characteristics are not found).

The fact is, that while Flindt and Binder correctly state that man has 312 anatomical characteristics strictly of his own, they fail to mention that he shares 396 with the chimpanzee, 385 with the gorilla, 261 with the orangutan, and 93 with the gibbon. These data were similarly made available by Keith (1911). Flindt and Binder chose to ignore it.*

A third and less well-known hypothesis, which has not been reviewed here, is one that can be referred to as the 'spore hypothesis'. This concerns the idea of micro-organisms being planted on Earth billions of years ago by extraterrestrials, and left to evolve to their present forms (Crick and Orgel 1973). Some writers have even combined the spore hypothesis with the hybrid hypothesis. With minimum data to work from, little can be stated about the spore hypothesis, other than to speculate on its likelihood.

One final observation is in order. None of the hypotheses examined above, nor any of the many other 'ancient astronaut' claims, have any direct bearing on the question of modern UFO

---

*There are several ways of interpreting the data provided by Sir Arthur Keith. The above figures represent this writer's interpretation, following consultation with others, who were unaware of the author's purpose. While different interpretations could result in different figures, these would still reflect the basic fact that man shares more anatomical and physiological characteristics with the apes than he possesses alone. Similarly, the new characteristics which have been identified in the ensuing seventy years do not alter these results.

reports. They represent two totally separate sets of data. Consequently, any attempt to solve one by explaining the other constitutes mere speculation.

ACKNOWLEDGEMENTS: The author wishes to thank James E. King, Professor of Primate Psychology, and Mary Ellen Morbeck, Professor of Human and Primate Evolution, both at The University of Arizona, for critical reviews of the original manuscript. The present article is the responsibility of the author only.

166

REFERENCES CITED IN APPENDIX

Cherry, Lorraine M., Case, Susan M., and Wilson, Allan C.
1978 'Frog Perspective on the Morphological Difference between Humans and Chimpanzees'. *Science*, Vol 200: 209–11.

Chiarelli, A. B.
1972 'Comparative Cytogenetics in Primates and its Relevance for Human Cytogenetics', in A. B. Chiarelli (ed.), *Comparative Genetics in Monkeys, Apes, and Man*. New York: Academic Press.

Clark, W. E. Le Gros
1963 *The Antecedants of Man*. New York: Harper & Row.

Cloudsley-Thompson, J. L.
1975 'Environment and Human Evolution'. *Environmental Conservation*, Vol 2: 265–9.

Crick, F. H. C., and Orgel, L. E.
1973 'Directed Panspermia'. *Icarus*, Vol 19: 341–6.

Dunn, F. L.
1966 'Patterns of Parasitism in Primates: Phylogenetic and Ecological Interpretations, with Particular Reference to the Hominoidea'. *Folia Primatologica*, Vol 4: 329–45.

Flindt, Max H., and Binder, Otto O.
1974 *Mankind – Child of the Stars*. Greenwich: Fawcett.

Fobes, James L., and King, James E.
1977 'Prosimian Sensory Capacities'. *Primates*, Vol 18 (3): 713–30.

Goodman, M., Koen, A., Barnabas, J., and Moore, G. W.
1972 'Evolving Primate Genes and Proteins', in A. B. Chiarelli (ed.), *Comparative Genetics in Monkeys, Apes, and Man*. New York: Academic Press.

Greenwell, J. Richard
1978 'Aridity, Human Evolution, and Desert Primate Ecology'. *Arid Lands Newsletter*, 8 (June): 10–18.

Hill, J. P.
1932 'The Developmental History of the Primates'. *Philosophical Transactions of the Royal Society*, Series B, 221: 45.

Hockett, Charles F., and Ascher, Robert
    1964   'The Human Revolution'. *Current Anthropology*, Vol 5: 135–47.

Keith, Arthur
    1911   Reply to Bonin. *Nature*, Vol 85: 509–10.

King, James E., and Fobes, James L.
    1974   'Evolutionary Changes in Primate Sensory Capacities'. *Journal of Human Evolution*. Vol 3: 435–43.

King, Mary-Claire, and Wilson, Allan C.
    1975   'Evolution on Two Levels in Humans and Chimpanzees'. *Science*, Vol 188: 107–15

Leroi-Gourhan, Arlette
    1975   'The Flowers Found with Shanidar IV, a Neanderthal Burial in Iraq'. *Science*, Vol 190: 562–4.

Miller, Dorothy A.
    1977   'Evolution of Primate Chromosomes'. *Science*, Vol 198: 1116–24.

Montagu, Ashley
    1964   Comment on Hockett and Ascher. *Current Anthropology*, Vol 5: 160–61.

Mooney, Richard E.
    1974   *Colony: Earth*. New York: Stein & Day.

Mooney, Richard E.
    1975   *Gods of Air and Darkness*. New York: Stein & Day.

Napier, John
    1970   *The Roots of Mankind*. Washington: Smithsonian.

Polyak, S.
    1957   *The Vertibrate Visual System*. Chicago: University of Chicago Press.

Solecki, Ralph S.
    1975   'Shanidar IV, a Neanderthal Flower Burial in Northern Iraq'. *Science*, Vol 190: 880–81.

Story, Ronald D.
    1976   *The Space-Gods Revealed*. New York: Harper & Row.

Story, Ronald D.
    1977   'Von Däniken's Golden Gods'. *The Zetetic*, Vol 2 (1): 22–35.

Strauss, W. L.

1936   'The Thoratic and Abdominal Viscera of the Primates'. *Proceedings of the American Philosophical Society*, Vol 76: 1.

Trench, Brinsley Le Poer
1960   *The Sky People*. London: Neville Spearman.

Trench, Brinsley Le Poer
1969   *Operation Earth*. London: Neville Spearman.

Trench, Brinsley Le Poer
1973   *Mysterious Visitors: The UFO Story*. New York: Stein & Day.

Von Däniken, Erich
1969   *Chariots of The Gods?* London: Souvenir Press

Von Däniken, Erich
1970   *Return to the Stars*. London: Souvenir Press (Later published in the United States under the title *Gods from Outer Space*.)

Von Däniken, Erich
1973   *The Gold of the Gods*. London: Souvenir Press.

Von Däniken, Erich
1977   *According to the Evidence: My Proof of Man's Extra-terrestrial Origins*. London: Souvenir Press.

Von Koenigswald, G. H. R.
1962   *The Evolution of Man*. Ann Arbor: University of Michigan Press.

Wilson, A. C., and Sarich, V. M.
1969   'A Molecular Time Scale for Human Evolution'. *Proceedings of the National Academy of Sciences*, Vol 63: 1088–93.

SELECTED BIBLIOGRAPHY

ON THE PRO-SIDE OF, OR WORKS SUPPORTING,
THE ANCIENT ASTRONAUT THEORY

Adamski, George. *Behind the Flying Saucer Mystery*. Original title: *Flying Saucers Farewell*. New York: Warner Paperback Library, 1961, 1967.

Bergier, Jacques. *Extraterrestrial Visitations From Prehistoric Times to the Present*. Chicago: Henry Regnery, 1970, 1973.

———— ed. *Extraterrestrial Intervention: The Evidence*. New York: Signet/New American Library, 1975.

Berlitz, Charles. *Mysteries From Forgotten Worlds*. Garden City, NY: Doubleday, 1972.

———— *The Bermuda Triangle*. Garden City, NY: Doubleday, 1974.

Binder, Otto O. *Flying Saucers Are Watching Us*. New York: Belmont, 1968.

Blumrich, Josef F. *The Spaceships of Ezekiel*. London: Corgi, 1974.

Bond, Bryce. Interview with Erich von Däniken. *Beyond Reality*, April 1974, pp57–62.

———— 'Erich von Däniken: He Believes in Space Men'. *Cosmic Frontiers*, November 1976, pp66–82.

Charroux, Robert. *One Hundred Thousand Years of Man's Unknown History*. Translated by Lowell Bair. New York: Berkley, 1970. Originally published in France under the title *Histoire Inconnue des Hommes Depuis Cent Mille Ans* by Robert Laffont, Paris, 1963.

171

Legacy of the Gods. New York: Berkley, 1974. Originally published in France under the title *Le Livre des Secrets Trahis* by Robert Laffont, Paris, 1965.

Masters of the World. Translated by Lowell Bair. New York: Berkley, 1974. Originally published in France under the title *Le Livre des Maîtres du Monde* by Robert Laffont, Paris, 1967.

The Gods Unknown. New York: Berkley, 1974. Originally published in France under the title *Le Livre du Mystérieux Inconnu* by Robert Laffont, Paris, 1969.

Forgotten Worlds. Translated by Lowell Bair. New York: Popular Library, 1973. Originally published in France under the title *Le Livre des Mondes Oubliés* by Robert Laffont, Paris, 1971.

The Mysteries of the Andes. Translated by Lowell Bair. New York: Avon, 1977. Originally published in France under the title *L'énigme des Andes* by Robert Laffont, Paris, 1974.

The Mysterious Past. New York: Berkley, 1975. Originally published under the title *Le Livre du Passé Mystérieux* by Robert Laffont, Paris, 1973.

Archives des Autres Mondes. Paris: Robert Laffont, 1977.

Chatelaine, Maurice. *Our Ancestors Came From Outer Space*, Garden City, NY: Doubleday, 1978.

Cohane, John Philip. *Paradox: The Case for the Extraterrestrial Origin of Man.* New York: Crown, 1977.

Collyns, Robin. *Laser Beams From Star Cities?* London: Pelham, 1975.

Creighton, Gordon. 'A Russian Wall Painting and Other "Spacemen"'. *Flying Saucer Review*, Vol 2, No 4, July/August 1965, pp11–14.

Dem, Marc. *The Lost Tribes From Outer Space.* New York: Bantam, 1977.

Dione, R. I. *God Drives a Flying Saucer.* New York: Bantam, 1973.

Is God Supernatural? The 4,000-year Misunderstanding. New York: Bantam, 1976.

Downing, Barry H. *The Bible and Flying Saucers*. Philadelphia: Lippincott, 1968.

Drake, W. Raymond. 'UFOs Over Ancient Rome'. *Flying Saucer Review*, Vol 9, No 1, January/February 1963.

    'Spacemen in the Middle Ages'. *Flying Saucer Review*, Vol 10, No 3, May 1964, pp11–13.

    'Space Gods of Ancient Britain'. *Flying Saucer Review*, Vol 11, No 4, July/August 1965, pp15–17.

    Gods or Spacemen? Amherst, WI: Amerst Press, 1964. Reprinted as *Messengers From the Stars* by Sphere Books, London, 1977.

    Gods and Spacemen in the Ancient East. London: Neville Spearman, 1973

    Gods and Spacemen in the Ancient West. London: Sphere, 1974.

    Gods and Spacemen in the Ancient Past. New York: Signet/New American Library, 1975.

    Gods and Spacemen Throughout History. London: Neville Spearman, 1975.

    Gods and Spacemen in Ancient Israel. London: Sphere, 1976.

    Gods and Spacemen in Greece and Rome. London: Sphere, 1977.

Flindt, Max H., and Binder, Otto O. *Mankind – Child of the Stars*. Greenwich, CT: Fawcett, 1962, 1974.

Fort, Charles. *The Books of Charles Fort*. New York: Henry Holt, 1941.

Ginsburgh, Irwin. *First, Man – Then Adam!* New York: Simon and Schuster, 1977.

Holiday, F. W. *Creatures From the Inner Sphere*. New York: Norton, 1973.

Hutin, Serge. *Alien Races and Fantastic Civilizations*. New York: Berkley, 1970, 1975.

Jessup, Morris K. *The Case for the UFO*. New York: Citadel Press, 1955.

    UFO and the Bible. New York: Citadel Press, 1956.

    The Expanding Case for the UFO. New York:

Citadel Press, 1957.

Kasântsev, Alexsandr. 'Prishel tsy iz Kosmosa?' (Visitors from Space?) Moscow: *SMENA*, September 1959.

'Did Ancients Meet Spacemen?' *Australian Flying Saucer Review*, Vol 1, No 3, September 1960.

'Vizitnye kartochi s stru'. (Calling Cards From Other Planets?) Moscow: *Tekhnika molodezhi*, No 1 1967, pp22–5.

Keyhoe, Donald E. *Aliens From Space*. Garden City, NY: Doubleday, 1973.

Kolosimo, Peter. *Not of This World*. New York: University Books, 1971.

Timeless Earth. New York: University Books, 1974.

Spaceships in Prehistory. Secaucus, NJ: University Books, 1976.

Krassa, Peter. *Erich von Däniken: Disciple of the Gods*. London: W. H. Allen, 1978.

Landsburg, Alan and Sally. *In Search of Ancient Mysteries*. New York: Bantam, 1974.

The Outer Space Connection. New York: Bantam, 1975.

Le Poer Trench, Brinsley. *The Sky People*. London: Neville Spearman, 1960.

Men Among Mankind. London: Neville Spearman, 1962.

Forgotten Heritage. London: Neville Spearman, 1964.

The Flying Saucer Story. London: Neville Spearman, 1966.

Operation Earth. London: Neville Spearman, 1969.

The Eternal Subject. London: Souvenir Press, 1973.

Secret of the Ages. London: Souvenir Press, 1974.

Leslie, Desmond, and Adamski, George. *Flying Saucers Have Landed*. London: Werner Laurie, 1953.

Lewis, L. M. *Footprints On the Sands of Time*. New York: Signet/
New American Library, 1975.

Michell, John. *The Flying Saucer Vision*. New York: Ace, 1967.

Mooney, Richard E. *Colony: Earth*. New York: Stein and Day,
1974.

         Gods of Air and Darkness. New York: Stein
and Day, 1975.

Navia, Luis E. 'In Defense of Ancient Astronauts'. *Fate*, Vol 29,
No 9, September 1976, pp63–9.

      A Bridge to the Stars. Wayne, NJ: Avery, 1977.

Norman, Eric. *Gods, Demons and Space Chariots*. New York:
Lancer Books, 1970.

        Gods, Demons and UFOs. New York: Lancer,
1970.

        Gods and Devils From Outer Space. New York:
Lancer, 1973.

Pauwels, Louis, and Bergier, Jacques. *The Morning of the Magicians*. New York: Stein and Day, 1964. Originally published
in France under the title *Le Matin des Magiciens* by Editions
Gallimard, Paris, 1960.

          Impossible Possibilities.
New York: Stein and Day, 1971. Originally published in
Germany under the title *Der Planet der unmöglichen Möglichkeiten* by Scherz Verlag, 1968.

        The Eternal Man. London:
Souvenir Press, 1972.

Pinotti, Roberto. 'Space Visitors in Ancient Egypt'. *Flying Saucer
Review*, May/June 1966, pp16–18.

Sanderson, Ivan T. *Uninvited Visitors*. New York: Cowles, 1967.

        Invisible Residents. New York: World, 1970.

        Investigating the Unexplained. Englewood
Cliffs, NJ: Prentice-Hall, 1972.

Sendy, Jean. *The Moon: Outpost of the Gods*. New York:
Berkley, 1968, 1975.

      Those Gods Who Made Heaven and Earth. New
York: Berkley, 1969, 1972.

      The Coming of the Gods. New York: Berkley, 1970,
1973.

Sitchin, Zecharia. *The 12th Planet.* New York: Stein and Day, 1976.

Spencer, John Wallace. *No Earthly Explanation.* New York: Bantam, 1974.

Steiger, Brad. *Atlantis Rising.* New York: Dell, 1973.

Steinhäuser, Gerhard R. *Jesus Christ: Heir to the Astronauts.* New York: Pocket Books, 1976.

Tarade, G., and Millou, A. 'L'enigma di Palenque'. *Clypeus,* October 1966, Vol 3, No 4–5, pp19–21.

Temple, Robert K. G. *The Sirius Mystery.* London: Sidgwick and Jackson, 1976.

Thomas, Paul. *Flying Saucers Through the Ages.* Translated by Gavin Gibbons. London: Neville Spearman, 1962.

Tomas, Andrew. *We Are Not the First.* London: Souvenir Press, 1971.

       The Home of the Gods. New York: Berkley, 1972, 1974.

Umland, Eric and Craig. *Mystery of the Ancients: Early Spacemen and the Mayas.* New York: Walker and Co., 1974.

Vallée, Jacques. *Passport to Magonia.* London: Neville Spearman, 1970.

Von Däniken, Erich. *Chariots of the Gods?* Translated by Michael Heron. London: Corgi Books, 1971. Published in hardcover by Souvenir Press, London, 1969. Originally published in Germany under the title *Erinnerungen an die Zukunft* (Memories of the Future) by Econ Verlag, Düsseldorf, 1968.

       Return to the Stars. Translated by Michael Heron. London: Corgi, 1972. Published in hardcover by Souvenir Press, London, 1970. Originally published in Germany under the title *Zurück zu den Sternen* by Econ Verlag, Düsseldorf, 1968.

       In Search of Ancient Gods. Translated by Michael Heron. London: Corgi, 1976. Published in hardcover by Souvenir Press, London, 1974. Originally published in Germany under the title *Meine Welt in Bildern* by Econ Verlag, Düsseldorf, 1973.

       The Gold of the Gods. Translated by

Michael Heron. London: Corgi, 1974. Published in hardcover by Souvenir Press, London, 1973. Originally published in Germany under the title *Aussat und Kosmos* by Econ Verlag, Düsseldorf, 1972.

    Miracles of the Gods. Translated by Michael Heron. London: Corgi, 1977. Published in hardcover by Souvenir Press, London, 1975. Originally published in Germany under the title *Erscheinungen: Phänomene die die Welt erregen* by Econ Verlag, Düsseldorf, 1974.

    According to the Evidence: My Proof of Man's Extraterrestrial Origins. Translated by Michael Heron. London: Souvenir Press, 1977. Originally published in Germany under the title *Beweise* by Econ Verlag, Düsseldorf, 1977.

Reply to 'Where von Däniken Went Wrong'. *Beyond Reality*, September/October 1977, pp8, 62.

    Im Kreuzverhör: Fragen aus Diskussionen rund um die Welt – Warren Götter auf der Erde? Erich von Däniken steht Rede und Antwort. Düsseldorf: Econ Verlag, 1978.

    'Why Do Critics Ignore The Positive Arguments For Ancient Astronauts?' *Second Look*, January 1979, pp12–13, 15.

Williamson, George Hunt. *Road in the Sky.* London: Neville Spearman, 1959.

    Other Tongues – Other Flesh. Amherst, WI: Amherst Press, 1952.

WORKS SCEPTICAL OF THE ANCIENT ASTRONAUT THEORY

Bainbridge, William Sims. 'Chariots of the Gullible'. *The Skeptical Inquirer*, Vol 3, No 2, Winter 1978, pp33–48.

Bord, Janet and Colin. 'Von Dänikenitis: A Tonic for Sufferers'. *Flying Saucer Review*, Vol 23, No 3, 1977, p29.

Bova, Ben. 'What Chariots of Which Gods?' *Astronomy*, August 1974, pp4–18.

Browne, Tisha. 'Revealed at last: The Truth About Space Gods'. *Titbits*, 13 April 1977.

Cohen, Daniel. *The Ancient Visitors*. Garden City, NY: Doubleday, 1976.

'Enoch and Other Cosmonauts'. *Time*, 22 February 1960, p26.

Ferris, Timothy. Interview with Erich von Däniken. *Playboy*, August 1974, pp51–2, 56–8, 60, 64, 151.

Ford, Barbara. 'Chariot of the Frauds'. *Science Digest*, December 1976, pp87–8.

Gadow, Gerhard. *Erinnerungen an die Wirklichkeit*. Frankfurt, West Germany: Fischer Bücherei, 1971.

Goran, Morris. *The Modern Myth: Ancient Astronauts and UFOs*. South Brunswick and New York: A. S. Barnes, 1978.

Graybill, Guy. 'Archaeologists View von Däniken'. *Pennsylvania Archaeologist*, Vol 45, No 3, September 1975, pp 37–9.

Gumnior, Helmut. 'Däniken & His Flying Machines'. *Encounter*, June 1977, pp44–6.

Hackler, Timothy. 'Is NBC Exploiting Creatures From Outer Space?' *Columbia Journalism Review*, July/August 1977, pp30–31.

Hughes, John. 'Chariots of the Clods?' *Playboy*, March 1975, pp117, 158–9.

Hugli, Paul. 'Where von Däniken Went Wrong!' *Beyond Reality*, May/June 1977, pp22–5.

Ley, Willy. *For Your Information: On Earth and in the Sky*. New York: Ace, 1967.

Lingeman, Richard R. 'Erich von Däniken's Genesis'. *New York Times Book Review*, 31 March 1974, p6.

Lorenzen, Coral E. 'Space Visitors – A Review and Comments'. *APRO Bulletin*, July 1962, pp 2, 5.

Meltzer, Edmund S. 'Swing Lower, Sweet Chariots of the Gods!' *Fate*, July 1976, pp34–42.

Miller, P. Schuyler. 'We Remember Arisia'. *Analog*, October 1974, pp170–75.

Oberbeck, S. K. 'Deus ex Machina'. *Newsweek*, 8 October 1973, p104.

Oberg, James. Interview with Erich von Däniken. *Ancient Astronauts*, September 1977, pp24–5.

Omohundro, John T. 'Von Däniken's Chariots: A Primer in the Art of Cooked Science'. *Zetetic* (renamed: *The Skeptical Inquirer*), Vol 1, No 1, Fall/Winter 1976, pp 58–68.

Ostriker, Alicia. 'What If We're *Still* Scared, Bored and Broke?' *Esquire*, December 1973, pp238–40, 328–30.

Peters, Ted. *UFOs – God's Chariots?* Atlanta, GA: John Knox Press, 1977.

Sampaio, Fernando G. *A Verdade Sobre Os Deuses Astronautas* (The Truth About the God-Astronauts). Porto Alegre a RS – Brazil: Editora Movimento, 1973.

Sheppard, R. Z. 'Worlds in Collusion'. *Time*, 2 August 1976, pp64–5.

Der Spiegel, editors of. 'Anatomy of a World Best-Seller'. *Encounter*, August 1973, pp8–17.

Story, Ronald. *The Space-Gods Revealed*. London: New English Library, 1977.

'The Leap of Faith' (letter to the editor). *Fate*, March 1977, p114.

'Von Däniken's Golden Gods'. *Zetetic*, Vol 2, No 1, Fall/Winter 1977, pp22–35.

Thiering, Barry, and Castle, Edgar, eds. *Some Trust in Chariots*. New York: Popular Library, 1972.

Von Khuon, Ernst, ed. *Waren Die Götter Astronauten?* (Were the Gods Astronauts?) Scientists Discuss the Theses of Erich von Däniken. Düsseldorf and Vienna: Econ Verlag, 1970.

White, Peter. *The Past is Human*. New York: Taplinger, 1974, 1976.

Wilson, Clifford. *Crash Go the Chariots*. New York: Lancer Books, 1972. Revised edition, San Diego, CA: Master Books, 1976.

The Chariots Still Crash. New York: Signet/ New American Library, 1975.

BIBLICAL COMMENTARIES

Asimov, Isaac. *Asimov's Guide to the Bible*, in two volumes. Garden City, NY: Doubleday, 1968.

Astley, H. J. D. *Biblical Anthropology*. London: Oxford University Press, 1929.

Boyd, Robert T. *Tells, Tombs and Treasure*. New York: Baker Book House, 1969.

Buttrick, George Arthur, ed. *The Interpreter's Bible*, in twelve volumes. Nashville, TN: Abingdon Press, 1952.

        ed. *The Interpreter's Dictionary of the Bible*, in four volumes. Nashville: Abingdon Press, 1962.

Gaer, Joseph. *How the Great Religions Began*. New York: Dodd, Mead & Co., 1956.

Keller, Werner. *The Bible as History*. Translated by William Neil. New York: William Morrow, 1956.

Magnusson, Magnus. *Archaeology of the Bible*. New York: Simon and Schuster, 1978.

May, Herbert G., and Metzger, Bruce M., eds. *The Oxford Annotated Bible with the Apocryhpa*, Revised Standard Version. New York: Oxford University Press, 1965.

Wright, G. Ernest. *Biblical Archaeology*. Philadelphia: Westminster Press, 1957.

HUMAN EVOLUTION AND THE ORIGIN OF INTELLIGENCE

Butzer, Karl W. 'Environment, Culture, and Human Evolution'. *American Scientist*, Vol 65, 1977, pp572–84.

Eiseley, Loren. *The Immense Journey*. New York: Random House, 1946, 1957.

        Darwin's Century. Garden City, NY: Doubleday, 1958, 1961.

Elliott, H. Chandler. *The Shape of Intelligence: The Evolution of the Human Brain*. New York: Charles Scribner's Sons, 1969.

Howells, William. *Mankind in the Making: The Story of Human Evolution*. Garden City, NY: Doubleday, 1967.

Isaac, Glynn. 'The Food-Sharing Behaviour of Protohuman Hominids'. *Scientific American*, April 1978.

Johanson, D. C., and White, T. D. 'A Systematic Assessment of Early African Hominids'. *Science*, Vol 203, 1979, pp321–30.

Leakey, Richard E. *Origins*. New York: E. P. Dutton, 1977.

        and Lewin, Roger. *People of the Lake*.

Garden City, NY: Anchor Press/Doubleday, 1978.

Marshack, Alexander. *The Roots of Civilization.* New York: McGraw-Hill, 1972.

McHenry, Henry M. 'Fossils and the Mosaic Nature of Human Evolution'. *Science,* Vol 190, 1975, pp425–31.

Napier, John. *The Roots of Mankind.* Washington, DC: Smithsonian Institution Press, 1970.

Rensch, Bernhard. *Homo Sapiens: From Man to Demigod.* New York: Columbia University Press, 1972.

Tobias, Phillip V. *The Brain in Hominid Evolution.* New York: Columbia University Press, 1971.

ARCHAEOLOGY OF MEXICO AND SOUTH AMERICA

Bennett, Wendell C., and Bird, Junius B. *Andean Culture History.* Garden City, NY: The Natural History Press, 1960, 1964.

Bernal, Ignacio. *The Olmec World.* Translated by Doris Heyden and Fernando Horcasitas. Berkeley, CA: University of California Press, 1969.

Brunhouse, Robert L. *In Search of the Maya.* New York: Ballantine, 1973, 1974.

Green, Merle. 'Classic Maya Rubbings'. *Expedition,* Vol 9, No 1, Fall 1966, pp30–39.

Hammond, Norman. *Mesoamerican Archaeology: New Approaches.* Austin, TX: University of Texas Press, 1974.

Hurtado, Eusebio Dávalos. 'Return to the Sacred Cenote'. *National Geographic,* Vol 120, No 4, October 1961, pp540–46.

La Fay, Howard. 'The Maya, Children of Time'. *National Geographic,* Vol 148, No. 6, December 1975, pp729–66.

McIntyre, Loren. 'Lost Empire of the Incas'. *National Geographic,* Vol 144, No 6, December 1973, pp729–87.

Rathje, William L. 'The Origin and Development of Lowland Classic Maya Civilization'. *American Antiquity,* Vol 36, No 3, pp275–85.

Robertson, Merle Greene, ed. *The Art, Iconography & Dynastic History of Palenque,* in three volumes. Pebble Beach, CA: Robert Louis Stevenson School, 1974, 1976.

Ruz Lhuillier, Alberto. 'The Mystery of the Temple of the

Inscriptions'. *Archaeology*, Vol 6, No 1, March 1953.

> *The Civilization of the Ancient Maya.* Cordoba, Mexico: Instituto Nacional de Antropologia e Historia, 1970.

Thompson, J. Eric S. *Maya Archaeologist.* Norman, OK: University of Oklahoma Press, 1963.

Von Hagen, Victor W. *Realm of the Incas.* New York: Mentor/New American Library, 1957.

> *The Aztec: Man and Tribe.* New York: Mentor/New American Library, 1958.

> *World of the Maya.* New York: Mentor/New American Library, 1960.

THE NAZCA LINES

Bridges, Thomas. 'Ancient Peru: The Mysterious Images of the Nazca Plains'. *New York Times*, 14 November 1976.

Davis, Emma Lou, and Winslow, Sylvia. 'Giant Ground Figures on the Prehistoric Deserts'. Proceedings of the American Philosophical Society, Vol 109, No 1, February 1965, pp8–21.

Gilbert, E. M. 'Roads to the Stars'. *Fate*, Vol 2, No 3, September 1949, pp60–65.

Isbell, William H. 'The Prehistoric Ground Drawings of Peru'. *Scientific American*, Vol 239, No 4, October 1978, pp140–53.

Kosok, Paul. *Life, Land and Water in Ancient Peru.* New York: Long Island University Press, 1965.

> and Reiche, Maria. 'The Mysterious Markings of Nazca'. *Natural History*, May 1947, pp200–207, 237–8.

> 'Ancient Drawings on the Desert of Peru'. *Archaeology*, Vol 2, No 4, December 1949, pp206–15.

Lanning, Edward P. *Peru Before the Incas.* Englewood Cliffs, NJ: Prentice-Hall, 1967.

McIntyre, Loren. 'Mystery of the Ancient Nazca Lines'. *National Geographic*, Vol 147, No 5, May 1975, pp716–28.

Moseley, James W. 'Peruvian Desert: Map for Saucers?' *Fate*, October 1955, pp28–33.

'Mystery on the Mesa'. *Time*, 25 March 1974, p92.

'Nazca Balloonists?' *Time*, 15 December 1975, p50.

Pinotti, Roberto, 'Siamo Extraterrestri'. *Clypeus*, April 1964, pp6–7.

Reiche, Maria. *Mystery on the Desert*. Privately published by the author, 7 Stuttgart-Vaihingen, Lutzweg 9, Germany, 1968.

Salzberg, Ruth F. 'Solving the Mystery of the Nazca Lines'. *Saga*, Vol 52, No 2, May 1976, pp32–3, 56–60, 62.

Woodman, Jim. 'New Mysteries in Ancient Peru'. *Braniff Place*, Vol 4, No 5, 1975, pp31–3, 42.

　　　　　　Nazca: Journey to the Sun. New York: Simon and Schuster, 1977.

ARCHAEO-ASTRONOMY or ASTRO-ARCHAEOLOGY

Allen, David A. 'An Astronomer's Impressions of Ancient Egypt'. *Sky & Telescope*, July 1977, pp15–19.

Del Chamberlain, Von. 'Prehistoric American Astronomy (*c* 1054 AD)'. *Astronomy*, Vol 4, No 7, July 1976, pp 10–19.

Eddy, John A. 'Probing the Mystery of the Medicine Wheels'. *National Geographic*, Vol 151, No 1, January 1977, pp 140–46.

Fell, Barry. *America B.C.* New York: Wallaby/Pocket Books/ Simon and Schuster, 1976.

Hadingham, Evan. *Circles and Standing Stones*. Garden City, NY: Anchor Press/Doubleday, 1976.

Hawkins, Gerald S. *Stonehenge Decoded*. Garden City, NY: Doubleday, 1965.

　　　　　　Beyond Stonehenge. New York: Harper and Row, 1973.

Hicks, Robert D. 'Astronomy in the Ancient Americas'. *Sky & Telescope*, Vol 51, No 6, June 1976, pp 372–77

Hitching, Francis. *Earth Magic*. New York: William Morrow, 1977.

Krupp, E. C., ed. *In Search of Ancient Astronomies*. Garden City, NY: Doubleday, 1978.

Michell, John. *Secrets of the Stones: The Story of Astro-archaeology*. Harmondsworth, Middlesex: Penguin Books, 1977.

'Once and Future Stars'. *Newsweek*, 19 December 1977, pp98–100.

'Stonehenge USA'. *Newsweek*, 24 June 1974, p60.

Technology Review, December 1977, special issue on 'The Astronomy of the Ancients' (various authors).

EGYPTIAN 'MYSTERIES'

Breasted, James Henry. *A History of Egypt*. New York: Charles Scribner's Sons. 1948.

Edwards, I. E. S. *The Pyramids of Egypt*. Harmondsworth, Middlesex: Penguin Books, 1947.

Emery, W. B. *Archaic Egypt*. Harmondsworth: Penguin, 1961, 1967.

Erman, Adolf, *Life in Ancient Egypt*. Translated by H. M. Tirard. London: Macmillan, 1894.

Fakhry, Ahmed. *The Pyramids*. Chicago: University of Chicago Press, 1961, 1969.

Flynn, Ruth M. 'The Myth of Pyramid Power'. *Fate*, Vol 31, No 4, April 1978, pp80–83. Reprinted from *New Horizons*, Vol 2, Pt 3, Issue No 8.

Gardner, Martin. 'Dr Matrix brings his numerological science to bear on the occult powers of the pyramid'. Mathematical Games, *Scientific American*, Vol 230 No 6, June 1974, pp116–21.

Glanville, S. R. K. *The Legacy of Egypt*. London: Oxford University Press, 1942.

Hall, Alice J. 'Egypt: Legacy of a Dazzling Past'. *National Geographic*, Vol 151, No 3, March 1977, pp293–311.

Maspero, G. *History of Egypt*, in nine volumes. London: The Grolier Society, 1906.

Mendelssohn, Kurt. 'A Scientist Looks at the Pyramids'. *American Scientist*, Vol 59, No 2, March–April 1971, pp210–20.

　　　　　　　The Riddle of the Pyramids. New York: Praeger, 1974..

Petrie, Sir Flinders. *A History of Egypt*, in five volumes. London: Methuen, 1896, 1924.

Steindorff, George, and Seele, Keith C. *Whdn Egypt Ruled the East*. Chicago and London: University of Chicago Press, 1942, 1957.

West, J. A. 'Pyramidology'. In *Man, Myth & Magic* edited by Richard Cavendish, Vol 17, pp2313–14. New York: Marshall Cavendish, 1970.

EASTER ISLAND

Casey, Robert Joseph. *Easter Island: Home of the Scornful Gods.* New York: Blue Ribbon Books, 1931.

Englert, Father Sebastian. *Island at the Center of the World.* Translated by William Mulloy. New York: Charles Scribner's Sons, 1970.

Finney, Ben R. 'Voyaging Canoes and the Settlement of Polynesia'. *Science*, Vol 196, No 4296, 17 June 1977, pp1277–85.

Heyerdahl, Thor. *Aku-Aku.* Londoh: George Allen & Unwin, 1958.

La Fay, Howard, and Abercrombie, Thomas J. 'Easter Island and Its Mysterious Monuments'. *National Geographic*, Vol 121, No 1, January 1962, pp90–117.

Mulloy, William. 'A Speculative Reconstruction of Techniques of Carving, Transporting, and Erecting Easter Island Statues'. *Archaeology & Physical Anthropology in Oceania*, Vol 5, No 1, April 1970, pp1–23.

'Contemplate the Navel of the World'. *Américas*, Vol 26, No 4, April 1974, pp25–33.

Routledge, Katherine (Pease). *The Mystery of Easter Island.* London: Printed by Hazell, Watson & Viney, and sold by Sifton, Praed & Co., London. Privately published by the author, 1919, 1920.

PIRI RE'IS MAP

Bagrow, L. *History of Cartography.* Revised and enlarged by R. A. Skelton. Cambridge, MA: Harvard University Press, 1964.

Davies, Paul C. W. 'The Piri-Reis Map: Fact and Fiction'. *Flying Saucer Review*, Vol 18, No 2, March–April 1972, pp 21–3.

Hapgood, Charles H. *Maps of the Ancient Sea Kings.* Philadelphia and New York: Chilton Books, 1966.

Keyhoe, Donald E. *Flying Saucers: Top Secret.* New York: G. P. Putnam's Sons, 1960.

Piri Reis Haritasi, Türk Tarihi Arastirma Kurumu Yayinlarindan: No 1. Istanbul: Devlet Basimevi, 1935.

ROCK PAINTINGS AND CAVE ART

Allen, Louis A. *Time Before Morning: Art and Myth of the Australian Aborigines.* New York: T. Y. Crowell, 1975.

Anati, E. *Camonica Valley.* New York: Alfred A. Knopf, 1961.

Colombel, Pierre. 'Old Frescoes Show Sahara Once Had Pleasanter Climate'. *Smithsonian,* Vol 6, No 4, July 1975, pp69–75.

Davidson, Daniel Sutherland. *Aboriginal Australian and Tasmanian Rock Carvings and Paintings.* Philadelphia: American Philosophical Society, 1936.

Eliade, Mircea. *Australian Religions.* Ithaca, NY: Cornell University Press, 1973.

Elkin, Adolphus Peter. *The Australian Aborigines.* Garden City, NY: Anchor Press/Doubleday, 1964.

Kühn, Herbert. *The Rock Pictures of Europe.* London: Sidgwick and Jackson, 1966.

Lajoux, Jean-Dominique. *The Rock Paintings of Tassili.* Translated by G. D. Liversage. Cleveland, OH: World, 1963.

Lhote, Henri. *The Search for the Tassili Frescoes.* Translated by A. Broderick. London: Hutchinson, 1959.

Marshak, Alexander. 'The Art and Symbols of Ice Age Man'. *Human Nature,* Vol 1, No 9, September 1978.

Ucko, Peter J. 'Cave Art'. In *Man, Myth & Magic: The Illustrated Encyclopaedia of the Supernatural,* edited by Richard Cavendish, Vol 3, pp429–34. New York: Marshall Cavendish, 1970.

Wellard, James. 'Rock Paintings'. In *Man, Myth & Magic.* Vol 18, pp2407–11.

GENERAL ANTHROPOLOGY AND ARCHAEOLOGY

Braindwood, Robert J. *Prehistoric Man.* Seventh Edition. Glenview, IL: Scott, Foresman & Co., 1964, 1967.

Bronowski, Jacob. *The Ascent of Man*. Boston, Mass: Little, Brown, 1973.

Ceram, C. W. *Gods, Graves, and Scholars*. Translated by E. B. Garside and Sophie Wilkins. New York: Alfred A. Knopf, 1967.

Cohen, Daniel. *Mysterious Places*. New York: Tower Books, 1969.

Coles, John. *Archaeology by Experiment*. New York: Charles Scribner's Sons, 1973.

Cornwall, I. W. *The World of Ancient Man*. New York: Mentor/New American Library, 1964.

Daniel, Glyn. *The Idea of Prehistory*. Harmondsworth: Penguin, 1962.

Daniel, Glyn and Paintin, Elaine, eds. *The Illustrated Encyclopaedia of Archaeology*. New York: Thomas Y. Crowell, 1977.

De Camp, L. Sprague, and Catherine C. *Citadels of Mystery*. New York: Ballantine, 1964.

De Camp, L. Sprague. *The Ancient Engineers*. Garden City, NY: Doubleday, 1973.

Dempewolff, Richard, ed. *Lost Cities and Forgotten Tribes*. New York: Pocket Books, 1976.

Farb, Peter. *Man's Rise to Civilization*. Revised 2nd edition. New York: Bantam, 1978.

Manners, Robert A., and Kaplan, David, eds. *Theory in Anthropology: A Sourcebook*. Chicago: Aldine, 1968.

Pelto, Pertti J. *Anthropological Research: The Structure of Inquiry*. New York: Harper and Row, 1970.

Ronan, Colin. *Lost Discoveries*. New York: McGraw-Hill, 1973.

Thorndike, Joseph J., Jr, ed. *Mysteries of the Past*. New York: American Heritage, 1977.

Watson, Patty Jo; Le Blanc, Steven A.; and Redman, Charles L. *Explanation in Archaeology*. New York: Columbia University Press, 1971.

MYTHOLOGY AND ANCIENT RELIGIONS

Barbour, Ian G., ed. *Science and Religion*. New York: Harper & Row, 1968.

Campbell, Joseph. *Myths to Live By*. New York: Viking Press, 1972.

Collins, John J. *Primitive Religion*. Totowa, NJ: Littlefield, Adams & Co., 1978.

Frankfort, Henri. *Kingships and the Gods*. Chicago: University of Chicago Press, 1948, 1978.

        et. al. *Before Philosophy*. Harmondsworth, Middlesex: Penguin Books, 1949, 1967.

Frazer, James G. *Folklore in the Old Testament: Studies in Comparative Religion, Legend, and Lore*. New York: Hart, 1975.

        The Golden Bough: A Study in Magic and Religion. New York: Macmillan, 1922, 1951.

Jung, Carl G., ed. *Man and His Symbols*. London: Aldus Books, 1964.

Lewinsohn, Richard. *Science, Prophecy and Prediction*. Translated by Arnold J. Pomerans, New York: Harper & Bros., 1961.

MacCulloch, John Arnott; Gray, L. H.; and Moore, G. F., eds. *The Mythology of All Races*. Boston, MA, 1914, 1932 (in 12 volumes).

Maranda, Pierre, ed. *Mythology*. Baltimore, MD: Penguin Books, 1972.

Murray, Henry A., ed. *Myth and Mythmaking*. Boston, MA: Beacon Press, 1959, 1968.

Vetter, George B. *Magic and Religion*. New York: Philosophical Library, 1958.

GENERAL COMMENTARIES ON CULT GROUPS AND PSEUDOSCIENCE

Cohen, Daniel. *Myths of the Space Age*. New York: Dodd, Mead, 1965, 1967.

Evans, Bergen. *The Natural History of Nonsense*. New York: Random House, 1958.

Evans, Christopher. *Cults of Unreason*. New York: Farrar, Straus & Giroux, 1973.

Fair, Charles. *The New Nonsense*. New York: Simon & Schuster, 1974.

Festinger, Leon; Rieken, Henry W.; and Schachter, Stanley.

When Prophecy Fails: A Social and Psychological Study of a Modern Group that Predicted the Destruction of the World. New York: Harper & Row, 1964.

Freedland, Nat. *The Occult Explosion.* New York: G. P. Putnam's Sons, 1972.

Gardner, Martin. *Fads & Fallacies in the Name of Science.* New York: Dover, 1952, 1957.

Goldenson, Robert M. *Mysteries of the Mind: The Drama of Human Behaviour.* Garden City, NY: Doubleday, 1973.

Hering, D. W. *Foibles and Fallacies of Science.* New York: D. Van Nostrand, 1924.

Jarvie, I. C. 'Cargo Cults'. In *Man, Myth & Magic: The Illustrated Encyclopaedia of the Supernatural,* edited by Richard Cavendish, Vol 3, pp409–12. New York: Marshall Cavendish, 1970.

Jastrow, Joseph. *Error and Eccentricity in Human Belief.* New York: Dover, 1962.

MacDougall, Curtis D. *Hoaxes.* New York: Dover, 1958.

Mackay, Charles. *Extraordinary Popular Delusions and the Madness of Crowds.* New York: Farrar, Straus & Giroux, 1972.

Petersen, William J. *Those Curious New Cults.* New Canaan, CT: Pivot Books/Keats, 1975.

Rachleff, Owen S. *The Occult Conceit.* New York: Bell, 1971.

Sadler, William S. *The Mind at Mischief: Tricks and Deceptions of the Subconscious and How to Cope With Them.* New York: Funk & Wagnalls, 1929.

Sladek, John. *The New Apocrypha: A Guide to Strange Sciences and Occult Beliefs.* New York: Stein & Day, 1974.

Tabori, Paul. *The Natural Science of Stupidity.* Philadelphia, PA: Chilton Books, 1959.

THE UFO PHENOMENON

Arnold, Kenneth, and Palmer, Ray. *The Coming of the Saucers.* Boise, ID. and Amherst, WI: Privately published by the authors, 1952.

Fuller, John G. *Aliens in the Skies.* New York: G. P. Putnam's Sons, 1969.

Gillmor, Daniel S., ed., and Condon, Edward U., scientific director. *Scientific Study of Unidentified Flying Objects*. New York: E. P. Dutton, 1969.

Hynek, J. Allen. *The UFO Experience: A Scientific Inquiry*. Chicago: Henry Regnery, 1972.

The Hynek UFO Report. New York: Dell, 1977.

and Vallée, Jacques. *The Edge of Reality*. Chicago: Henry Regnery, 1975.

Jacobs, David Michael. *The UFO Controversy in America*. Bloomington: Indiana University Press, 1975.

Jung, C. G. *Flying Saucers: A Modern Myth of Things Seen in the Skies*. Translated by R. F. C. Hull. London: Routledge & Kegan Paul, 1959.

Keel, John A. *UFOs: Operation Trojan Horse*. New York: G. P. Putnam's Sons, 1970.

Keyhoe, Donald E. *The Flying Saucers Are Real*. New York: Fawcett, 1950.

Flying Saucers From Outer Space. New York: Henry Holt, 1953.

The Flying Saucer Conspiracy. New York: Holt, 1955.

Flying Saucers: Top Secret. New York: G. P. Putnam's Sons, 1960.

Klass, Philip J. *UFOs – Identified*. New York: Random House, 1968.

UFOs Explained. New York: Random House, 1974.

Lorenzen, Coral E. *Flying Saucers: The Startling Evidence of the Invasion From Outer Space*. New York: Signet/New American Library, 1962, 1966.

Lorenzen, Coral and Jim. *Flying Saucer Occupants*. New York: Signet/New American Library, 1967.

UFOs Over the Americas. New York: Signet/New American Library, 1968.

UFOs: The Whole Story. New York: Signet/New American Library, 1969.

Encounters With UFO Occupants. New York: Berkley, 1976.

Abducted! New York: Berkley, 1977.

Menzel, Donald H. *Flying Saucers.* Cambridge, MA: Harvard University Press, 1953.

and Boyd, Lyle G. *The World of Flying Saucers.* Garden City, NY: Doubleday, 1963.

and Taves, Ernest H. *The UFO Enigma.* Garden City, NY: Doubleday, 1977.

Michel, Aimé. *The Truth About Flying Saucers.* New York: S. G. Phillips, 1956.

Flying Saucers and the Straight-Line Mystery. New York: Criterion Books, 1958.

Ruppelt, Edward J. *The Report on Unidentified Flying Objects.* Garden City, NY: Doubleday, 1956.

Sagan, Carl, and Page, Thornton, eds. *UFOs – A Scientific Debate.* Ithaca, NY: Cornell University Press, 1972.

Sanderson, Ivan T. *Uninvited Visitors.* New York: Cowles, 1967.

Invisible Residents. New York: World, 1970.

Saunders, David R., and Harkins, R. Roger. *UFOs? Yes!* Signet/ New American Library, 1968.

Tacker, Lawrence J. *Flying Saucers and the U.S. Air Force.* New York: D. Van Nostrand, 1960.

Vallée, Jacques. *Anatomy of a Phenomenon.* Chicago: Henry Regnery, 1965.

Passport to Magonia. Chicago: Regnery, 1969.

and Janine. *Challenge to Science: The UFO Enigma.* Chicago: Regnery, 1966.

The Invisible College. New York: E. P. Dutton, 1975.

Index

Abercrombie, T. J., 70n.

Abydenus, 106–7.

Adamski, George, 22, 131, 138: Biblical exegesis of, 131; interpretations of Ezekiel's visions, 131–2.

Aenarie, globe of fire seen in sky at, 102.

Aerial objects, plethora of, 101.

Aerial Phenomena Research Organisation (APRO), 141ff.; UFO cases and reports received by, 141ff.

Agrest, M. M., 22; early proponent of Space-god theory, 22.

Air Technical Intelligence Center (ATIC) US Air Force, 146.

'Airplanes', little gold, 92.

Alaparus, King of Babylon, 106.

Aldrin, Edwin, 18.

Alorus, King of Babylon, 106.

Amelon, King of Babylon, 106.

Amempsinus, King of Babylon, 107.

American Sign Language, 163–4.

Amillarus, King of Babylon, 106.

Ammenon, King of Babylon, 106.

Ancient Astronaut Society, 113n.

Ancient astronauts: concept of, 153; claims, 165.

Anementus, King of Babylon, 106, 107.

Angelucci, Orfeo, 132ff., 138: claims baptism and rebirth of flying saucer, 132; sees first flying saucer, 132–3.

Annedotus, King of Babylon, 106, 107.

Anodaphus, King of Babylon, 106.

Antikythera device, the, 91–2.

Apes: theories regarding, 154–5; chromosomes of, 158.

Appollodorus, 105, 106–7.

Apri, round shield seen in sky at, 101.

Ardates, King of Babylon, 107.
Argumentum ad ignorantiam, 53.
Ark of the Covenant, 40–1.
Armstrong, Neil, 18
Aruru, 110–11.
Ascher, Robert, 154.
Asimov, Isaac, 34–5, 44: suggests possibilities of cause of Sodom
· and Gomorrah's destruction, 34–5; works, *Asimov's Guide to the Bible*, 34q.
Astronomical, Journal, The, 121.
Audition, Evidence of in primates, 161.
Aurignacian period, 85.
Australopithecines, 47, 154.

Babylonia, 105ff.
Baghdad Batteries, 89n.
Banabas, J., 158.
Basilio, Ica artisan, 94.
Bergier, Jacques, 22; early proponent of Space-god theory, 22; works (with Louis Pauwels), *The Morning of the Magicians*, 22q.
Berosus, 104–5, 106.
Besant, Annie, 21, 22; early proponent of Space-god theory, 22.
Binder, Otto, 23, 153ff., 164–5: early proponent of Space-god theory, 23; arguments supporting hybrid hypothesis, 153ff.; 'mysteries' solved by explanation of extraterrestrial intervention, 154; works (with Max Flindt), *On Tiptoe Beyond Darwin*, 153q.
Blavatsky, Madame Helena Petrovna, 21, 22: founder of 'Theosophy' cult, 21; early proponent of Space-god theory, 22; works, *Secret Doctrine*, 21q.
Blumrich, Josef, 39, 44, 131–2: views regarding Ezekiel's visions, 39; works, *The Spaceships of Ezekiel*, 39–40q.
Brain, Evidence of in primates, 163.
Brecher, Dr Kenneth, 119; views regarding discovery of Sirius B., 119.
Bulfin, Robert L., Jnr., 125; works (with Richard Greenwell), *The Application of Technology in Developing Countries*, 114q.

Cabrera, Dr Janvier, 93
Cabrera stones, 92ff.
Cade, C. Maxwell, 98n.; works (with Delphine Davis), *The*

Taming of the Thunderbolts, 98n.

196

Proof of Man's Extraterrestrial Origins, 20q., 93q., 120q.:
Chariots of the Gods?, 15q., 17q., 31q., 33q., 40q., 46q., 56q.,
57q., 63q., 75q., 89q., 90q., 92q., 97q., 110q., 130q., 135q.; *In
Search of Ancient God:*, 70q., 103q.; *Miracles of the Gods*,
29n.q., 130q., 135q.; *Return to the Stars*, 46q., 47q., 58q., 60q.,
61q., 63q.; *The Gold of the Gods*, 46q., 65q., 92q.
Däniken, Otto von, father of Erich, 16.
Daos, King of Babylon, 106.
Davis, Delphine, 98n.; works (with C. Maxwell Cade), *The
Taming of the Thunderbolts*, 98n.q.
Dentition, Evidence of in primates, 159.
Dieterlen, Germaine, 119, 120, 121–2, 124, 125; works (with
Marcel Griaule), *African Worlds*, 122q., 124q.; *L'Homme:
Signas Graphiques Soudanais*, 124q.
Digestive System, Evidence of in primates, 158.
Digitaria star, 123–4; regarded by Dogon as smallest and heaviest
of all stars, 123.
Diodorus, 82.
Dogon peoples, 113: astounding astronomical knowledge of,
113; mythology, 114, 118, 122; particular knowledge of Sirius
system of, 114, 121; historical background, traditional myth-
ology and modern-day beliefs and practices of, 115–17, 119–20;
advanced culture of, 120–1; elaborate cosmological system of,
124; possible extraterrestrial contact with, 124–5.
Dogu statuettes, 87.
Drake, Walter Raymond, 23, 28, 29, 30–1, 42, 43: early proponent
of Space-god theory, 23; works, *Gods or Spacemen*, 28q., 29q.
Dunn, F. L., 159.

Easter Island, 69–75: location of, 69; statues on, 69–70; culture,
69.
Eddington, Sir Arthur, 119.
Egypt(ians): origins of people, 77; economy dependent on flooding of Nile, 78; building of Great Pyramid of Cheops by, 79–
81; pyramid building techniques of, 81–3; mummification by
priests, 83.
Eiseley, Loren, 47–9: explanation for comparatively rapid
development of human brain, 48–9; works, *Darwin's Century*,
48q., 49q.
Ellwood, Robert S., Jnr., 137.
Elohim, 30–1.
Eneugamus, King of Babylon, 106, 107.

Enkidu, man-like creature, 110–11.

Enoch, 33, 108.

ESP (Extra Sensory Perception), 16.

Ettinger, Robert C. W., 83: concept of mummification, 83; works, *The Prospect of Immortality*, 83q.

Euedocus, King of Babylon, 106, 107.

Euedoreschus, King of Babylon, 106.

Extraterrestrial(s): speculation, 10, 151; cross-breeding between e. and ape-men, 153.

Ezekiel, 39, 131.

Ezekiel's Wheels, 36–41; pertinent Bible verses relative to, 36–8.

Fakhry, Ahmed, 82, 84; works, *The Pyramids*, 82q.

Fayum period, 77.

Ferdon, Edwin, 74, 75; estimates amount of gold on Easter Island, 74.

Flindt, Max, 23, 153ff., 164–5: early proponent of Space-god theory, 23; arguments supporting hybrid hypothesis, 153ff.; 'mysteries' solved by explanation of extraterrestrial intervention, 154; works (with Otto Binder), *On Tiptoe Beyond Darwin*, 153q.

Florensky, Kirill P., 99, 100; leader of Tunguska expedition, 99.

Flying Saucer Review, 28, 103.

Fobes, James L., 160, 161.

Fordham, Frieda, 128, 137; works, *An Introduction to Jung's Psychology*, 128q.

Fort, Charles Hoy, 21, 22, 141; early proponent of Space-god theory, 22.

Freud, Sigmund, 127.

Genetic Biology, Evidence of among primates, 157–8

Giants, passages in Bible regarding g. quoted by von Däniken, 32–3.

Gilgamesh Epic, 110–11, 121

Giza, Great Pyramid of, 82.

Goodall, Jane, 50.

Goodman, M., 158.

Gorilla, 50; possible evolutionarily closer to man than chimpanzee, 158.

Grasp Response, Evidence of among primates, 161–2.

'Great Martian God of Jabbaren', finding of, 86.

Great Rift Valley System, 36.

Greenwell, Richard, 13, 114, 125, 154; works (with Robert L. Bulfin, Jnr.,), *The Application of Technology in Developing Countries*, 114q.

Griaule, Marcel, 119, 120, 121–2, 124, 125; works (with Germaine Dieterlen), *African Worlds*, 122q., 124q.; *L'Homme: Signes Graphiques Soudanais*, 124q.

Guggenheim, Dr Hans, 115.

Gusmão, Bartolomeu de, 63.

Hadria, men with white clothing seen in sky at, 102.

Hapgood, Charles H., 90n.; works, *Maps of the Ancient Sea Kings*, 90n.q.

Harkins, Arthur, 152.

Harland, J. Penrose, 44.

Heidel, Alexander, 112.

Helwan cloth, 89

Hercules, tales of, 121–2.

Heyerdahl, Thor, 73–4: expedition to Easter Island by, 73; describes carving, transporting and raising statues, 73; estimate of Easter Island population by, 74.

Hill, J. P., 162.

Hocket, Charles F., 154.

Homo erectus, 47, 154–5; intelligence of, 155

Homo habilis, 47.

Homo sapiens, 155; emergence of, 45.

Howells, William, 41–2, 44, 137: explains electrocution of Uzzah, 41; works, *The Heathens*, 41q.

Humanity, founding of, 46.

Hybrid Man theory, 164–5.

Hynek, Dr J. Allen, 149–50; expresses position on UFO problem, 150.

Hypothesis: hybrid, 153, 164; transplant, 153; spore, 165.

Icons, 42; suggestions frescoes relate to space-flight, 42–3.

Imhotep 81 and n.

Institute of Geological Sciences, 93.

Intelligence, Evidence of in primates, 163–4.

International Explorers Society, 62

Interplanetary spaceship theory, reasons for popularity of, 148.

Interpreter's Dictionary of the Bible, 32–3, 44.

Inversion layer as possible UFO 'explanation', 143.

Jaramillo, army captain, 66
Jason and the Argonauts, 121–2.
Jessup, Morris K., 19, 22, 24, 28, 30–1, 43: early proponent of Space-god theory, 22; studies of Maya tribe by, 24; account of Inca building of stone walls, 24ff.; publishes speculations on UFOs in Bible, 28; cites instances in Bible of UFOs, 30, 42; works, *The Case for the UFO*, 24q., 27q.; *UFO and the Bible*, 30, 42q.
Jesus Christ, 19, 42–3.
Jilek, Dr. Louise, 66: findings after trip to Cuenca regarding caves of gold, 66–8; criticises Erich von Däniken's naivety, 67.
Jilek, Dr. Wolfgang, 66; findings after trip to Cuenca regarding caves of gold, 66–8; criticises Erich von Däniken's naivety, 67.
Jung, Carl Gustav, 127, 134, 137, 138, 150: birth, 127; death, 127; career, 127; established Analytical Psychology school of thought, 127; theory regarding human psyche, 127; calls symbols of archetypes 'collective unconscious', 128; suspends judgment on reality or non-reality of UFOs, 129; invents 'gods' he needs, 129; works, *Flying Saucers – A Modern Myth of Things Seen in the Skies*, 127q., 128q.; *Psychological Types*, 127q.
Jupiter, 124; Galilean moons of, 125.

Kazântsev, Aleksandr, 22, 96, 98: early proponent of Space-god theory, 22; theory regarding Tunguska 'spaceship', 96–7, 98.
Keasler, John, 68.
Keith, Sir Arthur, 155–6, 164–5; lists number of characteristics of man, apes and monkeys, 155–6.
Keyhoe, Major Donald E., 147–8, 151: conclusions regarding 'flying saucers' mystery, 147–8; works, *The Flying Saucers Are Real*, 147q.
King, James E., 160, 161.
King, Mary-Claire, 157.
Koen, A., 158.
Kosok, Professor Paul, 61, 68; study of Nazca markings by, 61.
Krassa, Peter, 17.
Kronus, diety, 107.
Kubrick, Stanley, 18; views on constructing intriguing *scientific* definition of God, 18–19.
Kulick, Leonid A., 95ff.: belief Tunguska event caused by meteor, 96; craters found by, 98; finds minute grains of nickel-iron, 98.

La Fay, H., 70n.
Landsburg, Alan and Sally, 81n.; works, *In Search of Ancient Mysteries*, 81n.q.
Lanupium, fleet of ships seen in air at, 102.
Laurence, William, 34n; works, *Men and Atoms*, 34n.q.
Leakey, Louis S. B., 49.
Leakey, Mary, 49.
Leakey, Richard E., 49–50; works (with Roger Lewin), *People of the Lake*, 49q.
Lee, Stan, 9.
Leroi-Gourhan, Arlette, 155.
Leslie, Desmond, 22; early proponent of Space-god theory, 22.
'Levitation', 27.
Lewin, Roger, 49–50; works (with Richard Leakey), *People of the Lake*, 49q.
Ley, Willy, 142.
Lhote, Henri, 86; discovers 'Great Martian God of Jabbaren', 86.
Lhuillier, Alberto Ruz, 54–5; discovers secret tomb in Temple of Inscriptions pyramid, Palenque, 54–5.
Lindenblad, Dr Irving W., 121, 125; reports on speculations regarding possible third star in Sirius system, 121.
Literary Gazette, 33, 108.
Lorenzen, Carol and James, 141ff.: founder of Aerial Phenomena Research Organisation (APRO), 141; theories and opinions regarding UFOs, 141ff.
Lowell, Percival, 99; definition of comet, 99.

Magdalenian period, 85, 103; indications ancestors had seen UFOs, 103.
Mahabharata, myth reports flying vehicles and ancient atomic war, 104.
Mandala, symbol thought of by Jung as representing UFOs, 128.
Maria Auxiliadora, Cuenca, Church of, 65, 67.
Marquesas Islands, 69
Mars, Moon of, 89n.
Maruts, 'storm' or 'wind' gods, 104.
Maruyama, Magorah, 152.
'Mastabas', royal tombs, 81–2.
Maya(s), 56–8, 72.
McDonald, Dr James E., 143; views on atmospheric inversion, 143.
Megalarus, King of Babylon, 106.

Meharauli, Iron Pillar of, 89n.

Meidum, Pyramid of, 82.

Menger, Howard, 136–7, 138; claims earliest of contacts with outer space people, 136–7.

Menzel, Professor Donald, 142–3; explains alleged UFO happening as temperature inversion, 143.

Mesoamericans, 56.

Michel, Aimé, 102–3; discovers Magdalenian ancestors had seen UFOs, 103.

Michell, John, 23; early proponent of Space-god theory, 23.

Miller, Dorothy A., 158.

Millou, Andre, 55n.

Montagu, Ashley, 155.

Moon landing, historical, 18.

Mooney, Richard, 156: dismisses idea of cross-breeding or genetic manipulation, 156; proposes man placed on Earth 40,000 years ago, 156; questions appearance of hominids, 156.

Moore, G. W., 158.

Moricz, Juan, 65–6; cave expedition led by, 66.

Mount Palomar, 56.

Mummification: practice of, 83; preparing corpse for, 83.

Myth, contact, 108, 109, 114.

Napier, John, 163.

National Centre for Space Studies (CNES), 140; creates official government research group to study UFO phenomenon, 140.

Nazca, 60, 64: civilisation, 60; spaceport theory, 60–3; markings, 61–2; calendar theory, 61–2; grave-sites at, 62–3.

Neotony, Evidence of in primates, 162–3.

Ninsun, goddess, 110.

Nommo legend, 122, 124.

Nott, Julian, 63; flight over Nazca plain in primitive smoke balloon, 63.

Oannes legend, 104ff., 113–14.

Odacon, 107.

Olfaction, Evidence of in primates, 160–1

Olmec tribe, 57–8; sculpture carved by, 58.

Orgel, L. E., 165.

Oryana, 59.

OSC, 135–6.

Otiartes, King of Babylon.

Ovenden, Professor Michael, 120; statement regarding Dogon, 120.
Oxford Annotated Bible, The, 32, 39, 44.

Pacal, Lord-Shield, King of the Maya, 56.
Palenque 'astronaut', 54–6.
Palmer, Ray, 28; publishes *Gods or Spacemen?*, 28.
Parasites, Evidence of, in primates, 159.
Pauwels, Louis, 22: early proponent of Space-god theory, 22; works (with Jacques Bergier), *The Morning of the Magicians*, 22q.
'Period of the Round Heads', 87.
Peru, cotton in, 90.
Pesch, Peter and Roland, 120, 125; views on Dogon culture, 120–1.
Peters, Ted, 137n.; works, *UFOs – God's Chariots?*, 137n.q.
Pisco Bay, Trident of, 63–5; meaning of trident symbol, 64–5.
Plato, 128.
Pleides star cluster, 124.
Poher, Claude, 140
Polaris, star, 124.
Polyak, S., 160
Polyhistor, Alexander, 104-5, 106, 107: account regarding Oannes legend, 104–5; account of the great Deluge, 107.
Polynesians, 69–70.
Price, Derek de Solla, 92; detailed studies of the Antikythera device by, 92.
Primates: intelligence in, demonstration of, 50; intimate evolutionary linkages with man, 157, 161, 164; 'generalisation' of, 157; data provided to verify man's direct descent from p. ancestors, 157; Evidence of Genetic Biology in, 157–8; analysis and comparison of blood proteins of, 158; Evidence of Digestive System in, 158–9; similarity of alimentary tract of all p., 158–9; Evidence of Parasites in, 159; Evidence of Dentition in, 159; one of most important similarities with man – dental formula, 159; Evidence of Vision in, 159–60; exceptionally good colour vision in, 160; evolvement of stereoscopy and detail accuity, 160; Evidence of Olfaction in, 160–1; Evidence of Audition in, 161; Evidence of Grasp Response in, 161–2; Evidence of Reproductive Biology in, 162; Evidence of Neotony in, 162–3; Evidence of Brain in, 163; p. distinguishable from other mammals by increase in brain size, 163;

Evidence of Intelligence in, 163–4; extraordinary abilities in expression of true language shown by, 163; most advanced intelligence known to man exhibited by great apes, 164; conclusion all p. descended from common progenitors, 164; Sir Arthur Keith's data on number of individual characteristics of man and ape, 164–5.

Pulsars, 125.

Purdy, Ken, 147.

Pyramid-building techniques, 81ff.; intention as monuments, 82–3.

Quechan Indians, Rock Drawings of, 89n.

Quichuas Indians, Bolivia, 64–5.

Rameses II, mummy of, 83.

'Reciprocal altruism', 50.

Reeve, Bryant and Helen, 135, 138; works, *Flying Saucer Pilgrimage*, 135q.

Reiche, Maria, 68.

Re'is, Piri, maps of, 90–1.

Reiss, Otto F., 85n.

Reproductive Biology, Evidence of in primates, 162.

Rich, Valentin, 33, 108: suggests Biblical account of Sodom and Gomorrah possible literal description of nuclear explosion, 33; suggests Enoch's ascension into heaven interpreted as ride in flying saucer, 108.

Ridpath, Ian, 124, 126: states Sirius B orbits Sirius A in ellipse does not come from Dogon, 124; works, *Messages From the Stars*, 124q.

Ritual magic, 86

Rock paintings, 85, 87: subject matter for, 85; most famous of, 86.

Roggeveen, Admiral Jacob, 69; discovers Easter Island, 69.

Rome: form of ships seen in sky at, 101, burning shield passing over sky at, 102.

Rongorongo boards, 75.

Rorshach test, 10.

Rosetta Stone, discovery of, 77.

Rotundum, 128.

Routledge, Mrs Katherine, 72, 74, 75: expedition to Easter Island by, 72; observations on statues found on Easter Island, 73; works, *The Mystery of Easter Island*, 72q.

Roxborough, Ian, 119.

Ruppelt, Captain Edward J., 144, 146–7, 151: comments on 'flying saucer' reports, 146–7; works, *The Report on Unidentified Flying Objects*, 144q., 146q.

Sagan, Carl, 104, 108–9, 111, 112, 114, 119: suggests Oannes legend should receive more critical studies regarding extraterrestrial civilization contact possibilities, 104; works (with I. S. Shklovskii), *Intelligent Life in the Universe*, 104q., 109q.; *The Cosmic Connection*, 109q.

Sampaio, Fernando G., 13; works, *A Verdade Sobre Os Deuses Astronautas* (*The Truth About the God-Astronautas*), 13q.

Saqqara, Zoser's Step Pyramid at, 80–2; becomes first royal monument to be built entirely of stone, 81.

Sarich, V. M., 158

Saturn, rings of, 125.

Sendy, Jean, 23; early proponent of Space-god theory, 23.

Shaver, Richard S., 22; early proponent of Space-god theory, 22.

Shklovskii, I. S., 104, 109, 111, 112, 114; works (with Carl Sagan), *Intelligent Life in the Universe*, 104q., 109q.

Sigui festival, 118.

Sirius: binary system mystery, 78, 113–14, 117ff., 123; calendar based on rise of, 78; discovery of s. B, 113–14, 118–19, 121, 123; likely solution to mystery, 118; evidence of third star in system, 121.

Sisithrus (Xisuthrus), King of Babylon, 106–7.

Skeptical Inquirer, The, 14, 66.

Smith, Joseph, 130; founder of Mormon religion, 130.

Sneferu, King, 82; monument to, 82.

Sodom and Gomorrah, 33ff.: suggestion Biblical account might be nuclear explosion, 33ff.; evidence that destruction caused by earthquake, 35.

Solecki, Ralph S., 155.

Solutrean period, 85.

Space-god(s), 151; theory, 18–19, 24, 69, 137; proof of, 54.

Spoletum, globe of fire falls to earth at, 102.

Stingl, Professor Miloslav, 65.

Strabo, 35; comments on possible cause of destruction of Sodom and Gomorrah, 35–6.

Strauss, W. L., 159.

Sullivan, Walter, 112.

'Sun dog', 143.
Surya, 103–4.

Tarade, Guy, 55n.
Tarquinia, burning torch seen in sky at, 102.
Tassel, George W. Van, 135: founder of Ministry of Universal Wisdom, 135; allegedly contacted by 'Council of Seven Lights', 135; inventions of, 135.
Tassili 'Martian', 86–7.
Tellem population, 115.
Temple of the Inscriptions pyramid, Palenque, 54–6.
Temple, Robert K. G., 113–4, 118, 120ff., 125: claims regarding ancient knowledge of Sirius binary system, 113; researches into Dogon mythology, 114; creates impression Dogon isolated culture, 120; obsessed by hints of Sirius B anywhere and everywhere, 122; differences regarding Nommo legend, 122; works, *The Sirius Mystery*, 113q., 121q., 122q., 124q.
Thomas, Paul (pen name for Paul Misraki), 23; early proponent of Space-god theory, 23.
Tiahuanaco, Bolivia, 58–60, 64: culture of, 58–60; stonemasonry at, 59; Calendar, 89n.
Toffler, Alvin, 151.
Toltecs, 58.
Topkapi, 90
Trench, Brinsley Le Poer, *now* 8th Earl of Clancarty, 22, 28, 30–1, 42, 44, 153: early proponent of Space-god theory, 22; cites examples of UFOs in Bible, 30–1, 42; editor of *Flying Saucer Review*, 28; works, *The Sky People*, 28q., 30q.
Tunguska Event, the, 95–100.
Turolla, Count Pino G., 66; photographs taken of Padre Crespi's collection of 'priceless artifacts', 66.
UFOs (Unidentified Flying Objects), 10–11, 21, 30, 103, 139ff., 151: Carl Jung's interpretation as 'souls', 128; 'mystery' of 140; public opinion polls in USA findings regarding, 140–1; first wave of sightings, 146.
Utermann, Wilhelm (pen name: Roggersdorf), 15, 17.

Vallée, Jacques, 149, 150, 151: suggests UFOs may be part of 'control systems' influencing thoughts and behaviour, 149; works, *The Invisible College*, 149q.
Vedas, 103.
Venus, 124.

Verbal language, evolution of, 50
Vimanas, flying vehicles, 104.
Vision, Evidence of, in primates, 159–60.
Von Koenigswald, G. H. R., 162.

Walton, Travis, 145.
Watson, Fletcher G., 98: findings associated with Tunguska Event, 98; works, *Between the Planets*, 98q.
Weldon, John, 137n.; works (with Clifford Wilson), *Close Encounters: A Better Explanation*, 137n.q.
Wilkins, Harold T., 22, 23, 28, 101, 111; early proponent of Space-god theory, 22; his interest in UFOs, 23; reports examples of aerial objects observed, 101–2; works, *Flying Saucers From The Moon*, 23q.; *Flying Saucers on the Attack*, 23q., 101q.
Williamson, George Hunt (pen name for Michel d'Obrenovic), 22; early proponent of Space-god theory, 22.
Wilson, Allan C., 157, 158.
Wilson, Dr Clifford, 13, 40n., 137n.: works (with John Weldon), *Close Encounters: A Better Explanation*, 137n.q.; *Crash go the Chariots*, 13q., 40n.q.
Woodman, Jim, 62–3: produces evidence regarding Peruvians' knowledge of lighter-than-air flight, 62–3; works, *NAZCA: Journey to the Sun*, 62q.

'X-rated' type of art, 87.
Xesspe, Toribio Mexta, 61n.; discoverer of Nazca markings, 61n.

Zoser, King, 81. Step Pyramid of, 81.